THE DRAMA CLUB

THE DRAMA CLUB

Graduation

DENISE J SMITH

Queen Jungle Productions

CONTENTS

THE DRAMA CLUB
GRAUDATION

BY: DENISE J SMITH

| 1 |

WHO PULLED THE TRIGGER?

DEATH... A terrifying thought to many. Yet we stood side by side shaken, puzzled, mortified, helpless, as we stared death right in the eye. I then found myself wondering; *what's the point in life if it ends in death?* It was precisely 7:47 P.M. I know this because after fumbling around to take out my phone to use as a flashlight, I got a glimpse of the time. And though we were each called into the woods for different reasons that night, only one would bring us together in a way we'd never imagine. The sound of gunfire brought us so close that we could see and smell each other's breath as it blew quietly in the wind.

And as we slowly moved closer together, shaking from the trauma and chill of the night, there was a massive lack of trust amongst us as we blamed one another with condemning stares and stiff body pastures. Then suddenly, we were interrupted by the sounds of shouting and flashes of lights growing towards us as students and faculty rushed out of the side door of the gymnasium. Still haven't yet spoken a word to one another, we slowly moved around the body, which still had blood oozing out from the forehead. We then saw Principal Settle leading the crowd, staring right in our direction as she marched closer towards us. We looked down at the ground behind us, apprehensive of what would happen next. And as the lights from the flashlights grew brighter, we each stood our ground, waiting to shout our defense as Principal Settle came forward and stood just a couple feet away in dismay and barked,

"What in God's name are you all doing out here! And what was that popping? Were those gunshots? And why..."

Before Principal Settle could finish her thought, we watched as her eyes wandered in the one direction we feared. After noticing the body, I'm sorry, his body, Principal Settle became mystified as she tried to hold her composure. We each began speaking our defenses, stating that neither of us had anything to do with what just happened, that we were just as shocked as she was. The look on Principal Settle's face was nondescribable. We knew she didn't believe a word we were bellowing out.

"Move! And go stand over there! You can talk to the police when they get here!"

Principal Settle shouted for us to walk about ten feet to our right, away from the body. And while we stood next to a tree, watching as our classmates gawked at us from ahead, we began talking amongst ourselves.

"What did you do?" Josh whispered while eying Gabrielle and me.

"What did we do? No, what did you do? Everyone out here knows that you're the only one of us with any real motive! I bet if we searched you right now, we'd find the murder weapon."

"I don't have time for your bullshit! I can't afford to go to jail over something you did!"

"Wow! It really must be a bliss." I replied.

"Melanie, what the hell are you talking about? What must be a bliss?" Joshed barked.

"Your ignorance! I'm really becoming fascinated by it. Do you think that shouting delusions will convince everyone that you're innocent? It won't! But, I have a question, where did you go to earlier when you called yourself sneaking out of the gym?"

"That's none of your goddamn business!"

All eyes were on Josh. Crystal then asked,

"Wait...what is she talking about, Josh? And why is it none of our business?"

"Because she's lying! I-I don't know what she's talking about."

"Yes, you do, Josh! It makes perfect sense that it would be you. I can't believe it! Why?" Crystal asked in bewilderment.

"What the hell do you mean by why? I was standing right next to you when it happened!" Josh shouted.

"No, not the entire time! You stormed off right after calling me a whore, a slut, and everything else under the sun. You couldn't handle me being happy with someone else; you couldn't deal with it. And so what, was this your way of dealing with it? By hiding behind a tree and taking an innocent life? You're pathetic! Where's the fucking gun, Josh!" Crystal demanded.

"I don't know because I didn't do it! Christ, Crystal! Do you really believe that I would do this? Why aren't you blaming any of them? These people grew up around this crap. I didn't. I don't even know how to use a gun!"

"And because we're Black, you assume we do? I swear if someone else doesn't beat the ignorance out of you, I will!" I replied in a provoked manner.

Then out of nowhere, we were each startled when we heard,

"STOP! Just Stop! Please!"

The sound of Toni's voice breaking as he shouted out, pleading for us to listen, snapped me back into reality. He had been quiet until that very moment. And it took him crying out to get us to see that a human being just died! And instead of coming together to figure out why, we were placing blame and pointing fingers.

"He's dead! James is dead! Do you people care at all? I know that we all hate each other for whatever reason but Jesus! Can we take a few moments to be less selfish and try to figure out what the hell just happened without accusing each other? He was my friend, and now he's gone. He was a person, a living, breathing human being who was walking, talking just ten minutes ago. He wasn't something that didn't matter. He mattered, and he mattered to me."

It wasn't long after that when the sheriff, officers, and ambulance crew arrived. We watched as a few of the officers taped off the area while the others spoke to our teachers and chaperons. I then looked over at Gabrielle, who stood quiet and nervous. I wanted to comfort her, put my arm around her, but instead, I froze in fear. I just waited for her to put her hand in mine, nudge me closer, and ask,

"Did you see anything, Melanie?"

"No, did you?"

"No, but I felt something like someone was reaching for me...it spooked me."

"Are you serious? Who do you think it was?" I asked intensely.

"I don't know but, what if that was supposed to be me?"

"Nope, we are not even going to think like that. Whatever is going on had nothing to do with you and everything to do with them!" I replied, eyeing Josh and Crystal.

Shortly after, I noticed one of the officers approaching. We each halted our conversations and anticipated being hauled off in handcuffs in front of our entire senior class. When the officer finally approached, he looked at us and said,

"I'm Officer Lewis. Your Principal filled us in on what happened here tonight. But, unfortunately, what we don't have is the who and the why. So I suggest that for your sake, you be as honest as the truth will take you. But before you start flapping away, I'm going to have officer Green strip-search you one by one. Now, does either of you have any weapons on your person?"

We each just glared at one another, confused, horrified, and speechless. As for Officer Green, the darkness must have blinded me more than I realized because he appeared out of nowhere, gawking with his hands on his hips. As we continued to stand quietly, Officer Lewis prompted us to be honest one last time before losing his patience and saying,

"Alright...have it your way! Officer Green, why don't you start with that one, in the purple spandex!"

"Uhm, I have a name!" Toni interrupted.

The officers stared us down as we stood in a straight line, preparing to get searched. Officer Green then approached Toni while Officer Lewis continued to keep watch.

"What's your name? Do you have your I.D.?"

"Yes, and my name is Toni!"

Officer Green checked Toni's I.D. while blinding him in the eyes with his flashlight. The officer then confirmed that the person in the photo matched the person standing in front of him. After handing Toni back his I.D. Officer green continued down the line until he reached, Jesuse."

"Can you show me your I.D.?"

"Uh, yeah..."

After taking a minute to stare at the I.D., then back at the rest of us in the group, then back at the I.D. again, Officer Green motioned for Officer Lewis to walk with him about six feet away from us. We each watched as they quietly whispered amongst themselves. We weren't sure what to think as the two officers kept glancing back at us and talking. Their body language completely shifted. It was confusing to watch. I thought, what could be more severe than our dead classmate's body bleeding out behind our high school? Then seconds later, Officer Green and Officer Lewis rushed back towards us, and Officer Green said to Jesuse,

"The address on your I.D., is it correct?"

"Yes, why? What's going on?" Jesuse asked nervously.

"I'm going to need you to come with me."

Officer Green then took Jesuse away from the group and

walked him further ahead to where the other officers and student body were standing. I watched no I ogled as I tried to study the officer's body language to see what was happening. And as I continued to stare ahead, from the corner of my eye, I noticed that Officer Lewis was trying to strip search Josh. My attention diverted as Josh became highly hostile. I could see his chest pounding through his shirt. So, two things were happening simultaneously; one, Josh was throwing a complete temper tantrum, refusing to let Officer Lewis touch him. Then straight ahead, I saw Jesuse falling to the ground, breaking down in tears. The officers standing by tried to comfort Jesuse, but he refused as he shook them off and glared in our direction.

The look on Jesuse's face, the pain, the rage...it was dark out there in the woods, but there was enough light shining through to let me know that Jesuse was after blood! Jesuse then charged towards us while Josh was continuing to be Josh, refusing to allow Officer Lewis to strip-search him.

"Josh, would you stop! Just let him search you so we can all get out of here!" Crystal shouted.

"No, Crystal, I didn't do anything wrong! And it's my right as an American citizen, one who pays taxes in this goddamn country, not to be groped by a horny fucking cop."

"What taxes? Are you for real? You do realize that the only people who pay taxes are the ones who have actual jobs? And the only job you have is riding the bench for a losing football team," I replied.

"Look here, boy, if you won't cooperate with us, I'll take one hundred percent pleasure in putting you down on the ground myself." Officer Lewis replied.

Josh continued refusing as he took a step back with his pecs flexed, ready to challenge the officer. But before Officer Lewis could make a move, Jesuse was inches away with his fist, ready to attack. The officer following behind Jesuse tried her best to catch up as she shouted for him to *STOP!* I guess her short legs just weren't quick enough for Jesuse's powering sprint. And as I stood next to Gabrielle, I grabbed her hand and squeezed it tight while anticipating the loud blow and crackle to the jaw that would send Josh tumbling to the ground. What a mighty punch it was. Before Josh could properly land on the cold hard grass, Jesuse tackled Josh to the ground, then straddled himself on top and began turning his face into a bloody canvas. It wasn't long after that when the silver revolver came loose from Josh's pants and skipped across the grass.

Immediately, Jesuse stopped, pausing as he stared at the gun. Even the officers trying to detain Jesuse paused before continuing to separate Jesuse from the rest of the group. Jesuse then shouted out,

"There's the proof you need! He did it! He did it! He killed my mother!"

The rest of us stood there in shock, speechless. Josh then stood up and shouted,

"I didn't do it! It wasn't me!"

The female officer plus another officer grabbed Jesuse and took him away. Officer Lewis then carefully picked up the gun and said to Officer Green,

"Make sure that Forensics gets this. We'll need to see if this gun is a match for both crime scenes."

While Josh was tending to his wounds, Crystal softly asked,

"When can we go home? Are we going to be standing out here all night? It's freezing!"

"No, you won't be standing out here all night. But unfortunately for you five, your night is just beginning," Officer Lewis replied.

And although we wished that Officer Lewis was speaking figuratively, he was quite literal. Shortly after the action with Jesuse, the rest of us were brought in for questioning. Our night began with a series of questions, one right after the other. When it was my turn to be harassed by the twenty-one questions game, I was stumped. Time had fast-forwarded to 10 P.M., I had a migraine the size of Texas, and the blinding light hanging from the ceiling was not helping. I tried to be respectful, as respectful as I could be. But, I was sitting across the table from two police officers attempting to intimidate a lie out of me, which caused me to lose my patience.

"I don't understand. You saw who had the gun. Why are you questioning me like I was the one with the revolver in my back pocket?"

"This is just standard protocol. There were six of you out there. Surely you must have seen something?"

"I told you, for the twentieth time, it was dark. I have bad eyes, and I couldn't see anything!"

After giving my statement, there was a knock at the door. One of the officers sitting in the room got up to answer that knock. I examined his body language while he spoke to whoever was on the other side of the door. While hoping and praying that I would be free to leave, I heard the last words I expected to hear as the officer glared back at me and said,

"You're free to go!"

"Wait, so that's it?" I asked.

I was flabbergasted. I assumed the police must have finally gotten the truth out of Josh. After being reassured that I was free to go, I darted out of that room and didn't look back. Once I made my way back into the waiting area, I was surprised when I saw a familiar face waiting for me. I rushed over and grabbed the open seat next to her and said,

"Gabrielle! I was worried. Are you okay?"

"Yeah, I think so! No! Melanie, we just spent almost three hours here being questioned by the police. And James, James is dead! Why?"

"I don't know. It doesn't make any sense! None of it. And Toni..."

"He's a mess! I think the police are questioning him now."

"Wow! So, why do you think they're letting us go? Are we no longer suspects?"

"I guess, Melanie...I don't know. My dad is here. He's over there signing papers or something, I think."

I then glanced over at the desk to the right of me and noticed a tall, muscular male with blondish reddish hair speaking to one of the officers at the glass desk. I had never met Gabrielle's dad before then, but he looked exactly the way I imagined him. At first glance, he appeared standoffish and military-like, but underneath his tough exterior, I got the sense that he was just as scared as the rest of us. When Gabrielle's dad finally stepped away from the desk, I noticed someone else familiar standing on the other side of him. It was the last face I ever expected to see that night. She was holding her arms nervously as she waited for one of the officers to address her. My heart began to race; I was caught in a daze, for I knew that I was in trouble.

When I glanced back at Gabrielle, she was already out of her seat and leaving with her dad. Gabrielle then nervously turned around and waved goodbye as she got away. I wasn't bothered that she didn't introduce me to her dad; after all, we only shared our first kiss a few hours prior. The night that was supposed to change everything for the better instead just became another chapter to our never-ending nightmare. As I continued to watch Gabrielle walk away and turn the corner out the door, I felt a tap on the shoulder, and I quickly turned around.

"What are you doing here?" I asked with confusion.

"I'm here to take you home. Ms. Bailey asked me to pick you up."

I wasn't sure what to feel at that moment. I felt so many different emotions at once. I was grateful, embarrassed, but I think I was ashamed most of all. Seeing Ms. Bloom standing over me with that look in her eye, I felt my stomach drop into my uterus. I knew that she had to have been livid for several reasons. And yes, Ms. Bailey was out of town for a teacher's convention they were having up in Indianapolis. The one time she trusted me to be alone and this happened! I was sure I'd never be trusted to be alone again as I followed Ms. Bloom out to her car and hopped inside. I also knew I'd have a whole lot of explaining to do as well! So, as we pulled out of the parking lot, Ms. Bloom looked toward me and asked,

"So, how are you feeling?"

"Is it not obvious?" I replied.

"Right! I know that was a silly question, but you kids had no business being out there in the first place. And I hate what I'm about to say, but I'm relieved that it wasn't you! That doesn't take away from the fact of it being a tragedy that we lost one of our own."

Seeing Ms. Bloom glare at me with such concern rather than rage gave me hope. I felt that maybe I haven't entirely ruined things with her. Still, I had to ask,

"Do you think I did it?"

"What? Of course not! Why would you ask that?"

"Almost everyone else seems to think so. And it all happened out of nowhere! I didn't even realize how close James was to me. If I had been standing five feet closer, it probably would have been my body on an autopsy table instead of his!

"Well then, I guess it's a good thing you were standing five feet away."

And it wasn't just what she said, but it was the way she said it, her tone! I could hear the slight anger burrowing behind the concern. I couldn't tell whether or not she was secretly pissed at me, disappointed, or worried. I didn't want to worry myself about it. I just knew that I didn't want to be alone, especially after a night like that. So for the rest of the ride home, I worked up the courage to ask Ms. Bloom not to leave me alone. The ride was mostly quiet until we reached my neighborhood, and I asked,

"I don't want to be alone tonight. Is it okay if I stay with you?"

She paused before replying as if she was waiting for me to grovel, then said,

"I don't think that would be a good idea, Melanie. It's a school night."

"Please, I can sleep on the couch."

I gave her what she wanted, I begged, and I begged while waiting for her to pump the breaks and turn the car around. Ms. Bloom then slowly pulled the car over next to the curb in front of Ms. Bailey's house, turned toward me, and said,

"It's not just that it's a school night, Melanie. But, you made yourself very clear the other day about where you stand with me. What about Gabrielle? Can't you stay with her?"

The immediate pause following the shame that set in on my face was telling. How could I ask Ms. Bloom to take me in after what I did to her? There was nothing that I could say. The only thing I could do was stare ahead at the dark street and wait for Ms. Bloom to say,

"I see! Well, that's what happens when you get involved with little girls... Fine, Melanie, you can stay the night. I don't suppose you'll be going to school in the morning anyway after what just happed. But I need you to understand something; I'm not a doormat! If you expect to continue receiving special treatment from me, you're going to have to make a choice."

What could I say after all of that? I was so traumatized from the night that I didn't care what I had to do. I couldn't be alone, especially after knowing that there was still a killer out there. Ms. Bloom then turned the car around and drove us to her house. When we finally arrived and walked inside, she quickly offered me a change of clothes before getting ready for bed herself. After changing, I was ready to sleep on the couch, especially when Ms. Bloom went out of her way to hand me a blanket with a couple of pillows. But, after ten minutes of sitting in the dark on her living room sofa, my body slowly dragged me up the stairs to where Ms. Bloom was tucking herself into bed. I stood at the doorway, and she sat up, looked at me, and said,

"What are you doing, Melanie?"

"I can't sleep."

Ms. Bloom smiled and motioned for me to join her. I watched as she lifted her blanket and waited for me to crawl inside. It seemed that even when Ms. Bloom wanted to be angry with me, she couldn't deny her love for me. Lying on my left side, Ms. Bloom gently placed her arm around me as she cradled me closely. From the warmth of Ms. Bloom's body and the giant comforter that covered us, the chill in me started to recede. Though my body felt drained from the events that took place earlier in the night, my mind was still wide awake, trying to piece it all together. Everyone, including Josh, was free to go home. But how, why? Did the police not care that he had a gun? And on school property? I wasn't sure what to think. The only thing I could do was bask in the comforts of Ms. Bloom's bosom and let the night carry my thoughts away. That was until I pondered one final thought that; *if Josh wasn't the one who killed James, then who the hell did?*

| 2 |

JOSH

WHAT THE ACTUAL fuck just happened to my life? Jesus freakin Christ! I was at a loss for words! My brain was riding on a cloud of, what the fuck to fuck my life eternity. I know how this looks, I know what I had in my heart to do that night, but honestly, if that gangbanger hadn't shown up, I'm not sure I wouldn't have pulled the trigger. And it's a good thing he did show up, well, not for Jesuse, unfortunately, but if I pulled the trigger, my life would have been over! Thank God, though, that the police could verify that the gun I was packing wasn't a match for either crime. And more importantly, that it was still fully loaded. Whew!

However, that fully loaded gun didn't put me in the clear, not with the police and most certainly not with Jesuse. We were each still suspects in James's murder. And once the weekend had passed, I was right back at school on Monday morning with both of my parents, sitting in the principal's office.

"Listen, Ms. Settle, Principal, whatever...my son didn't do

anything wrong. You all should be begging us not to sue this damn school for negligence. My son could have been murdered right along with that boy and on your watch! I almost couldn't recognize his face two days ago! You're running a damn circus here!"

And here we go again, I said to myself. Though this time, I didn't so much disagree with my dad's argument. Principal Settle was trying her best to have me transferred to another school, and that we could not let happen!

"I do not have the time or the energy to argue with you, Mr. and Mrs. Fleming. I am dealing with an ongoing murder investigation, and I cannot have your son adding more stress to the situation. I am sure you're aware of the school's policy on weapons? Yes? Having possession of any weapons at this school is an automatic cause for expulsion!"

"I wasn't using it, I-I was keeping it for protection. That's it! And with everything that's been going on these days, can you blame me? The police even said that the gun wasn't a match. You can't just transfer me in the middle of senior year!"

"I can and will do whatever is necessary to keep this student body safe. I'm sorry, Josh, but you're out of strikes!"

My mother then interrupted with,

"I know that I have let my husband do most of the talking in the past, but now, it's my turn to speak. I agree that Josh is not a victim, and I apologize for his past and current behavior. However, if you're going to expel my son, I hope you plan to expel the rest of those students who were at that dance. The person responsible for the death of that poor boy is still walking around your halls. So you better be damn sure that you know what you're doing because we will take this to court if need be."

Wow! I didn't know she had it in her. I tried my best to keep a straight face; it took everything inside me not to crack a smile. But, my mother was right. Whoever killed James, they were still walking around free. And I, for one, was not going to sit back and take all the blame when I knew I was innocent. So, after my mother convinced Principal Settle to have a slight change of heart, I was released back to class with a warning.

"We will have security checking every and anyone who enters and exits the building. And Josh, if you get caught with anything that even resembles a weapon, your days at Lee Wallace High will be over! Do you understand?"

"Yes, ma'am!"

I tried to hurry my way out of the office, worried that something or someone would change her mind. The look on Principal Settle's face scared me most of all. Mostly because I still felt guilty for what I had in my heart to do that night. And I also knew that if Biscuit wasn't aware that I chickened out, I was confident he soon would be. *Pressure*, that's all I could feel as I walked down the hall to my locker to gather my books for first period. And just as I shut my locker, you know who showed up ready with a million questions.

"Dude? What the hell happened?"

"Not today Biscuit, just…not today."

I didn't even have the energy to try to suck up. My jaw still felt like a twelve-pound bowling ball had fallen on top of it. Damn, when Jesuse gets pissed off enough, he can release some hounds. After covering up my pain with some Tylenol, I made my way to my first-period class. As soon as I walked inside, I saw Toni and Melanie. *Great!* I sarcastically said to myself, what a fantastic way to start my morning! Before I could get comfortable in my seat, I heard Principal Settle call out over the intercom,

"Will, Josh Fleming, Toni Broussard, Melanie Howard, Crystal Spencer, and Gabrielle Davis, please come down to the principal's office immediately."

Damn! Here we go! I took a deep breath inhaling and exhaling before I stood up and made my way out of the classroom. I noticed Melanie glancing back at me, shaking her head in an accusatory manner as I walked by. I immediately took offense but tried not to take it personally. After all, I knew the truth. Then Toni got up out of his chair, wiping his invisible tears, making a scene. He was extra freaking dramatic. Whatever I just brushed past the two of them and made my way towards the principal's office.

One by one, we arrived in the waiting room and took a seat in whatever unoccupied chair we could find. Finally, after five minutes of awkward silence, Principal Settled called us into her office. The office was small and unneeded to say; six was a crowd. I quickly sat in one of the available chairs, and Toni sat in the other. Crystal, Melanie, and Gabrielle stood behind us as we waited to hear more bad news.

"I don't have much time so, I'll get right to the point. The five of you will spend the rest of the day in detention while I help the detectives try to figure out what happened Thursday evening. You will not look at nor will you socialize with any of the other students. As far as I'm concerned, you're ghosts! You don't exist! If you brought lunch, take it with you. If not, you will have lunch delivered to you. James Bernard's death will not fade away lightly; one of you is responsible, and I will find out exactly which one you that is! In the meantime, you will eat, sleep, and breathe detention. And when we're not watching you at school, you better believe someone will be watching you at home! Wherever you go, you will have eyes on you. Do you understand?"

I was still confused; I couldn't believe that I was still a suspect. But neither of us said a word as we shamefully nodded, *yes*, back at Principal Settle.

"Good! Ms. Bailey will come and take you to room 228. You will sit in there until we find a more permanent solution."

Seconds later, Ms. Bailey peeked her head inside and looked just as confused as the rest of us.

"Hi, I thought you wanted to see me? What's going on?" Ms. Bailey asked while staring at the five of us."

"I'm going to have Mr. Olive sub for you for the rest of the day. I need you to monitor these students in detention while I deal with this investigation."

"Excuse me?" Ms. Bailey asked.

This whole thing was preposterous. I could tell that even Ms. Bailey thought so by her blinding stare and firm hand placement on her hip.

"I cannot have these students near the rest of the student body causing more distress. And I apparently can't suspend or expel them either. So I have to keep them out of sight until I can figure something out! At best, this will only be through the end of the week."

"The rest of the week? I can't sit in detention for a whole week. I have cheer practice, and I don't know; let me see what else? A life!" Crystal blurted out.

"Then I suggest that you, or whichever one you who might know something, speaks up before Christmas break. Otherwise, you'll be spending the rest of your senior year in detention."

We each let out a long and defeated sigh following Principal Settle's statement. I could tell right away that it was going to be a dreadfully long week. It didn't seem like anyone knew anything, or at least no one wanted to be the first to speak on Thursday night's events. I was starting to become fed up with the situation. And yeah, I could have been more empathic, but I didn't know James. I was just glad that it was him instead of Crystal or me. But when I took a moment to see Toni and examine his body language, I was baffled at the fact that he appeared so emotionless. For someone who was crowned Drama Queen slash King for three years in a row, I found it odd that he couldn't even bring himself to form one wrinkle on his face. I mean, if I was in his shoes, I don't even think I could even get myself to get out of bed, let alone walk to school.

After Principal Settle convinced Ms. Bailey to babysit us, we followed her into room 228, adjacent to the theater. It was a small room with these old wooden desks. I guessed the room was part of the theater because it held clutter from ancient costumes and pieces of an old set. We each took a seat as we spread out as far away from one another as possible. Crystal was still so pissed at me that she refused to give me any kind of eye contact. I wasn't going to let her go on believing that I had anything to do with James's death. Once Ms. Bailey finally stepped out of the classroom, *to tinkle*, her words not mine, I blurted out,

"All right, you know what? I'm tired of you people acting like I'm some goddamn killer. I didn't do it! And if I have to repeat it a hundred more times, I will! You people don't think it's strange that he just shows up to school today, not showing any emotion at all? I mean, Toni, you're looking rather well with your fancy clothes and makeup all over your face! Why don't you save us all some time and open your big ass mouth and spit out the truth!"

I was beyond furious. I just wanted the nightmare to be over.

"Are you on crack? Leave Toni alone and go suck a thumb! You haven't learned anything from this, have you?" Melanie replied.

"Melanie, don't give into him. Just ignore him," Gabrielle replied.

"Whatever! You people are brain dead. I know it's not me! Clearly, it wasn't me. Which only means that it was one of you. And if you guys want to ignore the truth and spend the rest of the school year picking your noses while staring at each other behind a set, go right ahead. But, I'm going to tell the cops the truth. Because I know who killed James!"

"SHUT UP! You want me to say something? Do you want me to show more emotion? Here it is! You're scared! You want to bully me into talking so that you can feel better about the situation and be let off the hook! You can't even comprehend the fact that not everyone grieves the same way as you do. James was my friend. And no matter what happened in our relationship, I loved him. He didn't deserve to die in the woods behind our school like some rodent. But it wasn't me who killed him. So, sorry that I couldn't give you what you were looking for so that you can go back into the halls spreading your prejudice. It looks like you're going to have to sit tight and shut the fuck up like the rest of us."

"Fine! But we need to figure out what the hell happened that night. We need to start talking to each other. If neither of us did it, then someone out there did. Did anyone see anything?"

As I looked around the room to see if anyone appeared nervous or like they were withholding some kind of truth, I noticed Gabrielle. She caught my eye as I saw her nervously crossing her legs and wiping her forehead while glaring at Melanie. So I had to ask,

"Gabrielle, what did you see?"

"No! You're not going to do that. If you want to play detective, go home and pull out the Legos. We already spoke to the police!"

"Look, do you people want to solve James's murder or not?"

"And stop saying, YOU people?" It's offensive!" Melanie shouted.

"I wasn't even talking to you! So, why don't you let Gabrielle be a big girl and allow her to speak for herself? She saw something! So Gabrielle, and only Gabrielle, what did you see?"

After a minute of Gabrielle staring back and forth between Melanie and myself, she finally opened her trap and said,

"It wasn't what I saw... it's more like what I felt."

"Okay, so what did you feel?" I asked.

"I don't know; it felt like someone was pulling me. I was walking towards Toni, and then I couldn't see him anymore, and then, and then..."

"And then what!" I shouted.

"Gabrielle, you don't have to answer Josh's questions. Do you know why? Because he's not the fucking police!"

"Well, someone needs to be! I bet you all want this to fall on me, which is why you guys are just sitting on your asses, not saying anything. Well, guess what? That's not going to happen! So, if I have to play detective to get to the truth, then that's just what I'm going to do!"

"Josh, just give it a break. We will talk when we're ready. Just, ugh...can you be quiet for like, two minutes? Please!" Crystal interrupted.

Crystal sat there rubbing her hands on her lobes as if she developed a headache from my talking. *Fine*, I said. I shut my mouth and just sat there, letting the clock count down to the end of the day, just like the rest of them. If they weren't going to help me then I needed to figure it out myself. So I spent what time we had left in detention brainstorming. No matter how many ways I looked at it, I couldn't find a solution. It wasn't until the last bell sounded for the day that I was able to catch Crystal alone, away from the rest of them, and I begged her to speak to me. I had to chase after her down the hall just to get her to stop and talk.

"Crystal, please! Just…give me a chance to speak without storming away."

"What do you expect me to do, Josh? You made yourself very clear, Thursday night."

"What? Wait, is that why you've been acting like this? Avoiding my calls, avoiding me? You can't even look me in my eye right now."

"I can't look at you because I am completely disgusted by you. You lied to me when I asked you about the gun! And that shit you said about me in the woods, you never spoke to me like that before. All that crap about me being a traitor to my own race and that I was just desperate for some new dick? What the hell, Josh? I knew things were bad between us, but I would never stoop that low. How could you?"

The way Crystal glared at me with such disappointment, and hostility, I froze. I was speechless. But before Crystal could storm away again, I shouted,

"Wait… I'm sorry! The words were coming out of my mouth faster than I could control them. I didn't mean any of it!"

"You're always sorry, Josh! But, unfortunately, I have to go."

"Wait, where are you going? Let me give you a ride."

"No! That's okay because, where I'm going… you're most definitely not welcome."

Again, I let the love of my life walk out of my life. I started to follow behind until I was interrupted by the one and only,

Biscuit. I knew I wouldn't be able to blow him off a second time, so I slowly approached with a crooked smile.

"Hey man, sorry about earlier. It's just been a crazy weekend, you know?"

"Yeah, I do! I guess it's a good thing you didn't pull the trigger after all, huh? I mean, otherwise, we'd be having this conversation with a giant glass split in-between us."

My brain did a double-take. I didn't know what the hell he was saying. Until I thought, Biscuit must have found out that I didn't follow through with the plan. But then I wondered, how would he know? Who could have told him?

"What are you talking about?" I asked.

"I guess what I'm trying to say here is that...I know who pulled the trigger."

"Wait, huh? You saw what happened? Were you following me?"

"Come on, Josh! I needed to see for myself if you had it in you. But boy, was I disappointed to see that you not only failed me once but twice. I guess some of us just don't have the ball sack it takes to do the job."

I stood there bewildered, and I wondered, if Biscuit saw what happened, then why didn't he say anything?

"Well, if that's true, if you know who killed James, then why didn't you go to the police?" I asked.

"Joshy! How exciting would this all be if I went and did something like that? Oh, and by the way, you're out of the group! Yeah, you uh, you're just not the right fit for us. So, I guess I'll see ya around!"

"Wait! You can't just get rid of me. I didn't even get the opportunity to prove myself because someone beat me to it!"

"Just stop it, Josh! You're a pussy! It's okay to admit that."

And before emasculating me even more, Biscuit stepped closer and whispered,

"And from where I was standing, looks like you had plenty opportunity..."

With a wicked smile, Biscuit walked away, leaving me standing alone in the hallway, defeated. The entire time, I blamed Toni for killing James because he was the most prominent person to blame. But not once did I consider the fact that Biscuit himself could have been the one who got away. I mean, he's killed before; why wouldn't he do it again? But then again, if Biscuit was spying on me, if he was in the woods with us, why would he admit it? I figured that he wouldn't be that stupid, or maybe, hopefully...he was!

| 3 |

JESUSE & CRYSTAL

I COULD hear the sound of cool air whistling through the screen door as it loudly swung itself open and shut, sending goosebumps down my spine. It had been four days in a row now of me sitting in the corner of the living room, staring ahead at the scene where my mother died. I felt like I was living in one continuous nightmare, with added parts and characters. I just kept playing it all in my head; what did I do wrong? What could I have done to change the circumstance that found me?

I ignored all my sensibility along with each officer's repertory questions. They didn't understand, nor did they give a damn about my grief. They only pretended with a couple of dramatic frowns here and there or the occasional sigh of fake understanding. I didn't think anyone on Earth could understand my pain. I didn't think anyone could understand the loss, the emptiness, and the loneliness it feels not to have a single person in the world you can trust.

While watching them fumble around my house, I began thinking about how people really take for granted their relationships, the love, in their lives. I listened to one of the officers selfishly complain about his wife's nagging. He stated that he'd rather spend his time staring at me instead of being around someone who actually might enjoy the lingering gazes. It's annoying when people think they can sympathize with you by downplaying their happiness. But I strangely felt better when he and the other officers left me alone to my misery. That way, I could finally weep in peace without having to wear a mask. I often spoke about how important my mother was to me and how much her being alive dependent on me staying alive. But since actually losing the only person who kept me tethered to life, staying alive has become quite unbearable.

And while looking through the open blinds, I could see with my eyes that the sky was blue, but all I could feel inside was grey. The weather was calm, but I felt frozen in place, shivering as I cradled myself with my back against the wall. Then suddenly, out of nowhere, I heard a knock at the door. I figured it was the detective again; he would usually knock three times before inviting himself inside. However, this knock was different, gentle even, and with it, I heard,

"Jesuse? If you're in there, please open the door. You shouldn't be alone. I haven't seen you since Thursday night. I just want to make sure you're still breathing, at least."

I couldn't see her face, but I could hear her voice. I spent the past four days talking to myself about relationships, people, and love. And when I had the chance to be around those who could offer me comfort, I ignored them. I thought that if this is the effect of loving and being loved by someone, I decided I'd rather not.

"Jesuse, I know you're in there because I can see you sitting on the floor! Would you just talk to me?" She shouted.

As soon as I looked back up at the window, I was startled to see Crystal staring right at me. I felt my legs flinch as if my body wanted to get up to open the door, but the darkest part of my mind kept me glued to the ground. I couldn't stop myself from replaying the distorted image over and over of how my mother's face looked, covered in blood. I kept telling myself that it was just a terrible dream. But it wasn't. I even wished that I'd wake up and she'd be back sitting in her recliner smiling at me or yelling at me for something idiotic I've done. Instead, I just continued to stare at the yellow tape that surrounded the living room. And before I could take my next breath, I heard the front door loudly swing open and slam against the wall behind it as Crystal forcefully invited herself inside.

"Jesuse! Oh my God, Jesuse? Have you been sitting here this entire time?"

I appreciated the care and concern, but I wasn't in the right state of mind to converse with her.

"Jesuse, please, talk to me?"

Crystal continued begging me to talk, look at her, do anything other than staring at the wall like a vegetable. She then slowly sat in front of me, and as she examined my face and my clothes, she said,

"Jesuse, you look like you haven't had anything to eat or drink in days. I'm going to get you a glass of water and see what food you have in here, okay?"

I watched as Crystal got up, and I listened as she began to wrestle around in the kitchen, opening and closing cabinets and the fridge. Then I heard her shuffling around dishes as she prepared to make me something to eat. Minutes later, Crystal returned with a glass of water and a peanut butter and jelly sandwich.

"With all due respect, Crystal, I barely wanted to eat that shit when my mother was alive. I sure as hell won't be eating it now that she's dead!"

"Jesuse, you need to eat something. Just take a bite!" Crystal said as she tried to force-feed me.

I yanked my head away and squeezed my lips together so tight that they started to hurt. Then she tried with the water, and I shook my head once more. Crystal, however, stayed persistent. It wasn't until I finally opened my mouth that she got the message.

"Would you just STOP! I don't want to eat or drink any fucking thing. I want to die! Do you hear me? I want to die!"

I couldn't hold it inside any longer. I had planned to starve myself to death. The only way I'd move from my spot would be if the cops carried my body out on a stretcher.

"Don't say that, Jesuse. You can't keep doing this to yourself. I understand that you lost your mom…"

"No, Crystal…you don't understand! You can't possibly understand what I'm going through right now."

"You're right. I don't completely understand, and I'm so sorry that you have to go through this."

"Really? Because I told you…I fucking told you that I needed to be here. I should have been here watching over my mom instead of being hugged up with you at the stupid fucking dance. It's my fault she's dead! I should never have listened to you."

"No! I'm not going to let you do this. I'm not going to let you blame me, and I'm most definitely not going to let you blame yourself."

Crystal slowly sat next to me as she put the plate with the peanut butter and jelly sandwich to the side. With the glass of water still in her hands, she continued,

"I don't completely understand what you're going through, but I do know pain, and I do know loss. Your mom would not want you to through your life away; she would want you to live, to fight! Because you still have so much to offer the world. And you know what, you may not be able to see your mom right now, but she's here, in this room with us. And she would be very disappointed if you took away the one thing she has left of herself, her legacy. Jesuse, you are her legacy, and you can't give up."

For a moment, Crystal started to make sense. But, I couldn't shake the rage, the agony that lingered. I knew that my mother had AIDS and was dying, but I thought I'd have more time to… say goodbye. I thought I'd be more prepared. But, something I've quickly had to realize is that you can never fully prepare for death. No matter how much you plan for it in your head, the pain will hit you just as hard.

"I'm not going to go anywhere until you drink this entire glass of water and eat half of that peanut butter and jelly sandwich that I slaved in the kitchen to make for you!"

I don't know what came over me. Maybe it was Crystal's tone when she said it. But I did the one thing I thought I'd never do again, smile.

"Fine. I'll drink the water, but as of last Thursday, fuck the PB and J."

"Fine! I saw a can of Tomato soup in the cabinet. I will heat that up for you."

I watched as Crystal got up and walked into the kitchen. It's strange how much influence we humans have over one another. I mean, I was dead set on sitting in the same spot until all the power in me died out. But the tiny bit of love Crystal showed was enough for me not to give up.

Crystal spent the rest of the evening by my side, being supportive. She also made sure that I changed out of my four-day-old clothes and showered. After I showered and got redressed, Crystal asked me if I wanted to stay the night at her place. I wasn't ready to leave my house; even the police struggled to get me to leave. All I wanted to do was go back and sit in the same spot Crystal found me in, and that's what I did. After following me back into the living room, she said,

"Jesuse, you can't keep torturing yourself by sitting here staring at the damn recliner. Your home still looks and feels like a crime scene. Please, can you just get out for one night? I don't want to leave you here alone."

"Crystal, you don't get it… I can't leave! Ever since I came home and saw the police carrying my mom's body out on a stretcher, I haven't been able to leave. The amount of blood…Crystal, it was so much blood. My heartfelt like it was going to stop right then. My mom might be dead, but you're right, she's still here, and I'm never leaving her ever again."

After Crystal gave up on talking me into leaving, she begged me to let her stay. I didn't want to bring her down with me. I needed time and peace to grieve…. alone. When Crystal finally left, I grabbed a blanket from the closet and went back to my spot with my back against the wall staring ahead until I eventually fell asleep. I dreamt the most intense colorful dream ever. I was with my mom, and we were sitting on a bench at a park. She seemed so happy and at peace. I could feel her grabbing my hand. Her hand was so warm, and she smelled like sweet cherries. The part of the dream that shook me the most was feeling and seeing her so vividly. I've dreamt of many different people, even of Crystal, a few times. But even when I would dream of Crystal, she would always appear slightly different than reality, or she'd turn into Josh, which would really throw me off. But in this dream, my mom was perfect, without sickness or pain. She spoke to me as she placed her soft hand upon my face and whispered; *Sanctuary won't give you what you need, but courage will give you everything.*

I immediately woke up, shaking my head while trying to make sense of the dream. Then, as I glared out of the window, I became puzzled when I noticed that the sun was suddenly shining through, blinding me in the eyes! *It's daylight already?* I asked myself. Another thing I couldn't understand was time and how different it worked in the dream world versus the real world. There were times when I'd dream up an entire day but would have only been sleeping for a couple of hours. I may not be able to crack the science of the mind, but I did translate the message my mother sent me, and I was ready! I felt motivated for the first time since her death to leave the house. After getting dressed, I was ready to complete my quest, but first, I had to make a stop at Lee Wallace High.

When I say I was motivated, I mean I power walked down the street, to the school, and through the parking lot with sweat dripping down my forehead, *motivated*. However, the closer I got to the building, I became confused when I saw security checking backpacks at the front door and the long line that stretched to the sidewalk. It had been five days since the double shooting; I was so focused on what happened at my house, to my mother, that I momentarily forgot about what happened to James. However, as I approached one of the guards, memory quickly set in when Principal Settle charged toward me. After the guard patted me down not once but twice, I was finally clear to walk inside with Principal Settle as my escort.

"I'm surprised to see you here, Jesuse! With everything that's happened!"

"Yeah, well, I'm only here to get a few things out of my locker. I'll be out of your hair soon."

I continued walking down the hall with more eyes on me than a *Led Zeppelin* concert. Principal Settle continued to follow me with a confused look and said,

"Jesuse, why don't you come to my office so that we can talk in private?"

"Why? Is my presence causing too much of a disturbance for your liking?"

I shook my head as I finally approached my locker. After unlocking using my combination as quickly as possible, Principal Settled stood about two feet away and continued to speak,

"I just want to say that I'm deeply...deeply sorry for your loss. No one should ever have to live through the horrors you're living through right now. I'm here for you, Jesuse. We all are."

"Thanks, but I got what I needed. You no longer have to keep watch."

I stood there, angrily waiting for Principal Settle to disappear. Still, instead, she continued to linger around like an unwelcomed nat.

"I've already added your grievance time; you have up to two weeks in addition to winter break. I want you to know that we are here to support you in any way we can."

"Thanks, but I won't be needing any special favors or your pity. Life has other plans for me, and I think high school is no longer a part of that plan. But uh, I appreciate the concern."

After sarcastically smiling goodbye, leaving Principal Settle speechless, I walked down the hall toward the same faces that continued to gawk, pissing me off even further. Before making my way back towards security, I ran into the last person on Earth I needed to see, Josh. He just stared at me with a look of confusion and then excitement. And Crystal was disappointingly by his side, looking more shocked than I expected her to be. My mind, however, was focused on something more important, I didn't have the time to try and figure out what she was doing with him, so I kept walking. Crystal then shouted out,

"Jesuse, w-what are you doing here? And where are you going?"

Crystal tried running after me. I wasn't sure what I was more pissed over, being back in that building or seeing her with Josh. Watching the two of them together made my blood boil hotter than the hottest summer day in Arizona.

"*Jesuse*, stop for a minute?"

"What, Crystal?" I asked sternly.

"What do you mean, *what?* I could barely get you to take a step out on your porch yesterday, and today you're here?"

Josh approached with curious eyes. I didn't want to give him the satisfaction of watching me fall apart, so I tried to play it cool. However, calm was the complete opposite of what came out of my mouth.

"I see a lot more has changed around her besides the new security," I replied while glaring back and forth between the two of them.

"Josh and I are headed to detention. It's where they're keeping us for the rest of the week."

"So, just you two? Why didn't you mention this yesterday?"

"No, it's not just Josh and me. It's everyone! Everyone who was there that night. Jesuse, I didn't mention it because it wasn't important. Come on, don't be like that."

"Yeah, well, you two have fun. I got to go!"

It was too much for me to feel embarrassed. I left without saying another word. Only leaving Crystal with the pain from my expression as I questioned her intentions and walked out of the building.

I COULDN'T understand what was going through Jesuse's mind most of the time. The last thing I needed was for him to worry himself over Josh and me. I guess I'm sort of late to the introductions, but I'm sure you've already formed some opinion about me based on what you've learned so far? Don't! You don't know me! Only what you might think you know, or your preconceived ideas and biases. People say there are two sides to every story; I believe there are three, my version, their version, and the truth. Josh and I have known each other since we were kids, and we've been together on and off for six years. We were back at the off-again stage, and he's been trigging very hard to wiggle himself into the on-again stage. But it was going to take a lot more than empty promises and tears to win back my affection. And before you even formulate it in your brain, NO, I wasn't using Jesuse, nor have I ever. I just, well, Jesuse melted a different part of my heart, a piece that's been extremely difficult to ignore. And Josh, he's always held the other half of it. That was until recently.

Josh and I continued down the hall when he forcefully said,

"I don't know what you see in the guy."

"Jesuse has heart...an important ingredient for making kind humans, something you sadly lack!"

I left Josh speechless, that was until we made our way to detention, which had mysteriously moved to the auditorium. After walking inside, I noticed Melanie, Gabrielle, and Toni huddled up in a corner sitting towards the front of the stage. Josh then blurted,

"Hey, I have heart, plenty of heart! Which is why it's been difficult for me to…"

"Difficult to do what? What, Josh?"

"Nothing, forget it!"

"No, Josh, I want to know what you're talking about?"

"If I tell you, you have to swear that you won't say anything to anyone!"

I agreed not to tell a soul so that he'd calm down and spill the beans. After we finally took our seats in the middle aisle about seven rows up diagonal from the rest of the gang, Josh hesitantly opened his mouth while I anxiously waited for him to say,

"I think it was Biscuit. No, I'm like 90 percent sure that it was him."

"Josh, what the hell are you talking about?"

"I'm talking about James! Hello?"

It took a moment for me to gather my thoughts and piece together the nonsense Josh was spitting out at me. After wiping my face and inhaling and exhaling from the level of annoyance I had built up, I regrettably decided to ask another question,

"Are you telling me that you think Biscuit is responsible for James's death?"

"Uh, yeah! He practically confessed it yesterday. I had no choice; I had to go to the police."

"Wait a minute. You did what? And what exactly did Biscuit say to you?"

Before I was able to take in more of Josh's nonsense, Ms. Bailey walked inside, and as she approached, she blurted out,

"Good morning! I understand that it's been a tough couple of days for you all. And just so that I'm not shouting across the auditorium the entire time, I'm going to need you all to scoot in closer before I begin."

Ms. Bailey watched as she waited for us to move closer. We each just looked around at each other until Ms. Bailey shouted, demanding that we sit in the same aisle of the auditorium. *Great!* Not only did I get to be annoyed by Josh and his imagination, but I had to sit next to the three Black Stooges! Well, two and a half, since Gabrielle is part African American. Anyway, the three of them moved closer and sat two rows in front of Josh and me. Then Ms. Bailey continued to speak.

"Thank you, that's better. I hope we won't have to deal with each much longer and that things will go back to normal by the end of the week. And if you're wondering why you've been moved here to the auditorium. It's because the classroom is being used for an actual class today. And with the auditorium being the only room open, this is where you'll remain for the rest of the week.

"Now, I do have a few rules; rule number one, no swearing! I consider this auditorium to be a safe haven away from the outside world. I like to think of it as my heaven, and on stage, I play God. And God doesn't tolerate evil!"

"Did she just compare herself to God?" I quietly asked Josh.

"Rule number two; No talking when I am talking! That's what I won't tolerate! Rule number three, be respectful! Be respectful, not only to me but to each other as well. You might not see each other out there, but in here, you're family."

Before Ms. Bailey could continue adding to her made-up list of rules, Josh interrupted and blurted out,

"So, excuse me, your highness, just curious here. What happens if we don't follow these rules? I mean, the only reason we are in here is because Principal Settle needs to hide us away from the rest of the school. It's not like we can be suspended or expelled."

"Oh, on the contrary. You might not be able to suffer any kind of consequences for Thursday night's brutality yet! But believe me when I say, if you so much as sneeze the wrong way in here, you'll go right back to the principal's office. All she needs is one excuse. Now, if you want to interrupt me again and give Principal Settle that excuse, then, by all means, go right ahead."

The look on Josh's face was embarrassing enough for both of us. Sometimes I don't understand why he opens his mouth.

"Now then, to my final rule...do your homework! Your teachers will drop by your syllabuses soon, and until then, find a book or something to read to keep yourselves occupied."

Damn! And I used to think she was the nice one. So after waiting for a second to see what Ms. Bailey would do and two to five seconds of awkward exchanges between her and myself, I decided to take out a magazine. Ms. Bailey then announced that she'd be in her office, and as soon as she turned the corner, our mouths ripped open while Josh went back to playing detective.

"Anyway, like I was saying before, I think Biscuit's the who did it! At least that's what I told the police."

"Why would you do that? You know that he's going to kill you, no murder you, right?"

"Biscuit won't do a damn thing because he'll be too busy sitting his ass in a prison cell getting dipped in gravy!"

"You're a complete dumbass. You know that too, right?"

"It's either him or me. And it damn sure won't be me!"

"What is your proof, Detective?"

"My proof is his confession! He told me that he was in the woods with us that night! Crystal, you think he followed me in the woods just to stare? He's a freaking murderer! He followed me behind the school, and he even followed me to…"

And then it happened. My confusion quickly turned to curiosity as I waited for Josh to finish his sentence. But instead, he held his head down in shame and turned away from me. I immediately knew something wasn't right, that he was hiding something.

"No, you don't get to spit eight ounces of fluids my way and then just leave me in suspense. So, where did Biscuit follow you to? And come to think of it, because you so eagerly brought it up, where the hell did you go during the middle of, *Single Ladies?*"

"What?" Josh asked.

"The SONG! It was playing when you randomly tried and failed to sneak out. I saw you. What aren't you telling me?"

I raised my voice, not purposely but instead out of vexation. After my little outburst, I noticed that the voices of the three stooges became silent while they tried to eavesdrop.

"Hold on, Josh. Uhm, excuse me?"

I leaned forward to get the rest of the group's attention. Melanie, Gabrielle, and Toni each turned around in that exact order, and I continued to say,

"I hope that you three aren't snooping in on my conversation. Because whatever Josh and I are talking about is none of your concern. So why don't you turn back around and continue your discussion about the final season of, *The L Word*, or whatever the hell it is that you watch!

"Whoa! A bit overprotective, aren't we?" Melanie interrupted.

"And, nobody was listening to your conversation, Crystal. Your voice was just so loud that it disrupted our conversation about the final season of *Beverly Hillbillies*." Gabrielle added.

"Damn...good one!" Melanie instigated.

Then out of nowhere, Toni got out of his seat to give everyone a piece of his mind.

"I don't get you, not a single one of you. It's been five days since James died, and I'm the only person in this room, the entire building who cares! You all only care about yourselves and your problems. And Josh, the only thing you care about is not getting a conviction. But I actually hope they find the person responsible so I can sleep better at night. I know that I'm innocent. I don't need to shout it a million times a day to convince everyone around me that I am."

Toni then slowly sat back in his seat, and Josh just had to open his mouth again, stirring the pot.

"Toni, if you're doing this to prove a point because of what I said yesterday, don't. We all know that James was a loony. He treated you like shit. That's why I figured someone in your shoes would be relieved."

"Relieved? Everyone in this room is carrying around a bucket of secrets. James went through things you could never understand. He needed help, support! Not death. And now he'll never get that chance to change, to become the person he was meant to be. And, if you know something that the rest of us don't, then speak up! Otherwise, shut the hell up!"

I was surprised to hear the way Toni spoke about James. It made me think of my situation with Josh. As I said, we had been seeing each other on and off for the past six years. There were even times when I felt I hated him, but underneath that hate was so much love. He just makes it hard to get to it sometimes. But I knew that Josh was hiding something from me. I could feel it! Another ten minutes passed before we were each handed our syllabuses for the day, time dragged on from there, and it sucked! However, when the day was finally over, I walked out with Josh, expecting he would give me some part of the truth, anything! But instead, he played it off and danced around the subject.

"It was a mistake, Crystal! You know how sometimes your brain jumbles up words, well, that's what happened to me."

Josh and I continued walking down the hall while I pressed the subject further.

"No, I'm not talking about that anymore! I'm talking about the fact that I saw you leave. Where did you go?"

"To take a piss!"

"No, you're not being honest with me. You're not telling me the truth. What did you and Biscuit do? God...did you go to his house that night? Is that where you called yourself sneaking off to?"

"Whose house?"

"Jesuse's house, Josh! Did you... I can't believe I'm even asking this but did you two have anything to do with his mother's death? And do not lie to me!"

I waited as Josh and I stopped in the middle of the hallway.

I could see his face tensing up, his fists clinching from nervousness. My heart raced the longer I waited for him to open his mouth. I was positive that Josh knew something he wasn't telling me. Then right when he was about to speak, right when I was about to get my truth delivered from his chapped white lips, Biscuit and two officers approached.

"You sick twisted son of a bitch...I can't believe you'd lie on me just to cover your ass." Biscuit shouted.

"I don't know what you're talking about," Josh calmly replied.

The two officers who had Biscuit in handcuffs tried to escort him out of the building, but Biscuit's strength compared to theirs wasn't even a match. Biscuit just continued to lash out while holding the two officers off.

"I'm a fucking suspect now because you told them I was in the woods with you clowns that night... that I planted the gun on you? Seriously? It was fully loaded when they found it! They're not going to get shit on me!"

"Don't make us have to throw you on the ground and carry you out of here!" Said one of the officers.

Biscuit just continued to ignore them as he said,

"You're just doing this because I eliminated you from the group. Well, you can try to come up with as many lies as possible just to pin this whole thing on me. But I promise you, if I go down, you're going down with me. Only one of us stepped foot inside that house, and we both know which one of us that was. Good luck explaining that one to the police! You better pray I get a charge! You better pray hard!"

Biscuit and the two officers finally walked off, leaving everyone in the halls watching in shock. I didn't know what to think, what to believe. Josh had this look of fear, embarrassment, and shame even. But I didn't care. It was time for him to tell me the truth.

"I'm going to ask you one more time, Josh. Where did you go during the middle of the dance Thursday night?"

For the first time, Josh was speechless. It was right then that I had my answer, and I didn't want to know more.

"You know what, I don't even need to hear it. Your silence says it all."

"I didn't do it…I swear Crystal…it wasn't me," Josh replied.

"No, I know it wasn't you. What I don't know is why you were at Jesuse's house and with Biscuit!"

I felt so many emotions flowing through me at once. I couldn't even finish my thought. I shook my head in shame as I took one last look into Josh's eyes before walking away. Josh tried calling out to me, but I continued to ignore him. I held back my tears because I felt one more look at him would result in a downpour. I thought I could trust him. We were eleven years old when we first met during recess at the playground. Josh has lost his way since then. He became someone I couldn't even recognize. Through all the frustration and confusion, a small part of me believed Josh would never be capable of taking another life. Or maybe he was, and I didn't know him as well as I thought.

Furthermore, as I made my way out of the building to the parking lot, I was surprised to see that my mom showed up. She was loud and proud as she stood by the passenger door, shouting for me to hurry my way towards her. I love my mother dearly, I do, but that woman drives me up the wall. She's the kind of mother who doesn't give a shit about what people think of her. At least she does an excellent job of hiding it. My mom also has a strong voice, with a tiny bit of hoarseness from all the years of smoking, making it very distinct in a crowd. As she continued to wave me down, impatiently waiting for me to reach her green Jetta Volkswagen, I hid my embarrassment as I walked past the crowd of students. Once I was within talking distance, I tried to hush my mom into the car before she could embarrass me further.

"Mom? What are you doing here? And, what the hell are you wearing?"

I glared at my mother wearing a silky green short sleeve shirt covered in yellow ducks, and then I moved my way to her highly tight green yoga pants. Yeah, my mom knew how to stand out in a crowd.

"Honey, I told you a week ago that I would be picking you up so that you can keep me company. Remember? I'm getting my first Botox injections today, and I'm nervous! I'm also thinking about doing a little something to the derriere. You know... I need to keep things exciting for your daddy in the boudoir!"

"Ewe! Okay, mom, that's enough! I don't even want to imagine whatever the hell it is that people over fifty do in the boudoir! So, just, no sex talk, please!"

"Well, your dad and I can do everything and probably more than what your generation is capable of doing these days. It's just unfortunate that you kids lack imagination."

"Mom, STOP!"

Oh my God! I mean, seriously! I didn't want to know any of that! I adored how my mom and I could talk about anything, but she needed to learn some boundaries. After another five minutes of being mortified, I finally got my mom to change the subject. She asked about my day and if they ever caught the *Dark Night Killer*, as she liked to call it. I explained that the investigation was still ongoing, and I was afraid of what the truth might reveal. My mom could tell that I became slightly distant after the conversation, which I did. I lied and said that I was okay because I didn't want to tell her what I knew about Josh and how he could be involved with not just one murder but two.

Once we made it to the appointment and got checked in, my mom suggested that she'd make an appointment for me as well. That's when I felt every single blood cell in my body zip line to my face, and I snapped!

"Why would you even suggest that?"

"Crystal, it's a part of being a woman. You have to do certain things to maintain and or enhance your beauty. I mean, Jesus Crystal, your ass is flatter than my pancakes. Don't you want to be sexy, have guys drooling over you? You don't want Josh to grow bored of you, do you?"

"I didn't realize that I needed a big ass to be sexy!"

"And here we go with the dramatics. I was just suggesting that you get some injections to make your lips plumper. You have a beautiful face and a skinny body; it doesn't hurt to add a little extra oomph. These young girls, they're all doing it. There's nothing wrong with *keeping up with the Kardashian's*, so to speak."

Mothers…. Got to love them, right? We've been having these conversations since I was a little girl. If I ever had high self-esteem, you can thank my mother for chipping away at it year after year. The sad thing about it is that I knew she meant well. I just wished that she found the beauty she was given, that she passed down to me, to be plenty or more than enough. But, you can't have it all, I guess. Anyway, I sat with my mother until her very last injection. Once it was time to go home, I had the thought to call Jesuse. I hadn't heard from him all day and was concerned. I wasn't even sure if Jesuse and I were still a thing. It was kind of hard to talk about, you know, with him losing the person he loved most in the world.

When my mom and I finally made it home, she settled in upstairs with my dad, and I went to call Jesuse to let him know that I was coming back over. It was around 6:00 pm when I decided to sneak out. Once I arrived at Jesuse's house, I was disturbed by how dark it was on his front porch. After knocking three times, he finally answered with the door cracked just enough for me to see his face, and then he rudely said,

"Hey, what are you doing here?"

"I told you that I was coming by not even thirty minutes ago... what's going on?"

"I told you not to come; you shouldn't be here."

"And I told you that I was coming over anyway. Can I come in?"

Jesuse hesitated; I could tell. I didn't understand why he was so secretive or what he was hiding. Once Jesuse finally opened the door, I was shocked when I stepped into further darkness. I didn't know whether to freak out and run or to stay and call for help.

"Jesuse, why is it so dark? You don't even have your porch light on."

"Yeah, well, the electricity was cut off. My mom was supposed to pay the late bill yesterday, but you know, with her being dead now and me not having access to shit, we lost power."

I was disturbed by Jesuse's living conditions. I knew there was no way he could continue living in a house without power. He didn't even have a job. And I thought to myself; *how would he support himself?* There was no way! But this time, I needed to be more assertive in getting him out of the house.

"You cannot keep living like this. Come on. You're coming with me."

I reached for Jesuse's arm, trying to nudge him towards the front door, and he quickly yanked himself away from me, causing me to lose my balance and almost fall.

"What the hell is wrong with you? Listen, I understand that you're grieving right now, but you cannot stay in this house without power!"

"I'll light a candle." Jesuse dryly replied.

"I'm not laughing, Jesuse. You don't have a job. You don't have any food, any electricity. I mean, look at this place…"

I continued on my rant as I tried to prove to Jesuse how unlivable his condition was. I stormed my way into the kitchen, opening and slamming every empty cabinet to prove my case. Which was that he couldn't survive off of just canned soups and old bread. As I continued moving through the kitchen, searching for a candle, a flashlight, anything, I was startled by what I found hidden in the pull-out silverware drawer next to the sink. My heart dropped. I became frightened, then triggered as I glared deep into his drawer and quietly asked,

"What the hell is this?"

"Get out..."

Jesuse charged toward me, slamming the drawer shut, ordering me to leave. I refused.

"No! I want you to tell me what the hell you're doing with a gun in your kitchen drawer? What is wrong with this town and guns?"

"I need you to leave, Crystal, now!"

"What do you plan on doing with this? Where did you even get it from?"

"I can't do this with you right now. Please, go..."

"I'm not going anywhere until you talk to me and tell me what is going on!"

I refused to let Jesuse deal with his pain alone. I worried about his health, physically and mentally. I stared as he continued to fidget around the kitchen, shaking his head as if he was wrestling with the idea of telling me what he harbored in his heart. I just wished I could step inside his mind; I wished I could understand his thoughts so that I could somehow get through to him and talk some sense into him. But, just when I thought Jesuse was about to open up to me as he leaned back against the refrigerator, he instead begged me to leave one last time.

I COULDN'T tell Crystal what my plans were. I couldn't confess to her that the only reason I went back to school was to retrieve the bracelet I had stolen from Josh's house. And the only reason I kept it in my locker was becasue I knew it would be the one place too prominent that Josh would think to look. He was clever enough to get me to empty my backpack but not clever enough to check the pockets of my pants. His mom never even noticed it was missing, so I thought. That's beside the point; the point was that I was saving this little secret for a rainy day. The bracelet was only worth seven hundred bucks. I used six hundred of that to buy a Glock 17 off of this dude from the corner. The rest of the money I kept for emergencies, like food. There's no way I could look her in the eye without slipping up. Crystal kept begging me to talk, begging me to leave with her. I knew that the only way I could get Crystal to back off would be to make her cry, and so I tried,

"I'm not your burden or your class project! You don't get to tell me how to grieve. It's my grief, not yours! And I don't have the time or energy to entertain you. So just go be with Josh, someone who needs you, because I don't need you!"

"Wow! Do you really think that?"

The look in Crystal's eyes broke me even more. Surprisingly because I thought there was nothing else left in me to break. I had to stand firm; I needed Crystal to give me time alone. After walking towards the front door and waiting for Crystal to walk through, she did. But not before tripping over one of my mother's old books, which caused her to loudly bump her shin on the low sitting wooden coffee table.

"Damn it, Jesuse! You can try to shut me out all you want, but I don't scare that easily. So I will respect you for now and give you the time and space you need to grieve while also praying like hell that you're not planning to do something stupid. But Christ, come Monday, and you're still fiddling around in the dark, you'll need more than a few hurtful words to get rid of me."

And just like that, she was gone. Part of me was grateful to have someone like her in my corner, someone who didn't give up on me as quickly as most. Unfortunately, the other part of me didn't give a damn about who was in my corner. I was focused on getting revenge and was willing to do whatever necessary to make sure that I succeeded. I couldn't focus on a relationship, friends, or enemies. Well, maybe one enemy. My mother's murder had Fernando's name written all over it. It took me a minute to figure it out, but I finally remembered what he meant by; *then we'll be even*. No one else could have done this; no one else had the motive. And no, I didn't trust the police; I didn't trust them to deliver me proper justice. I wanted to be the one who looks Fernando in the eye right before he takes his last breath.

After walking back into the kitchen, I grabbed the gun from the drawer and gently placed it in the palm of my hand. I examined the gun with the help of the moon glaring light in through the kitchen window. You get a feeling of satisfaction, control, and even power from holding such a weapon. So as I held on tight and pointed towards the wall, my heart pounded with excitement as I imagined turning Fernando's face into a bowl of strawberry-covered grits!

POW!

| 4 |

TONI

DEAR GOD, *is it just Wednesday?* That's what I asked my-self first thing in the morning as I walked down the horrid halls of Lee Wallace High. I noticed I seemed to have started a new trend called *Black Widows*. Everywhere I turned, every student and teacher I saw was wearing black. Though I, of course, was a lot more fashionable in my black silky blouse and pants. Out of respect to my late James, I told myself that I'd dress in nothing but black for the entire week. Black socks, black shoes, back nails, black lipstick, black everything! And I know I wasn't married to James and that he was the worst boyfriend in history, but he took a large piece of me to heaven or hell with him. And he also left a large part of himself here with me.

The halls were quiet, too quiet; in fact, I didn't know what to do with my freedom as I power strutted my way into the boy's restroom. *At last*, I said to myself as I looked around without a jock or KKK member to be found. I then took a deep breath while glancing in the mirror before taking a mo-ment to touch up my eyeliner. I anticipated the sound of the door creaking as I waited for someone to barge inside, and they did, right before saying,

"Oh, sorry! I didn't think there would be anyone in here..."

The boy just stared my way, wearing bright orange eyeliner, a V-neck t-shirt, and tacky tan skinny jeans. And don't get me started on the hair; it stood straight up like a porcupine, with blonde highlights.

"You're fine, honey! Though I don't think I've ever seen you before. What's your name?" I asked.

"I'm Sarah, with an H... I'm a freshman. I've seen you around a few times."

"Oh really? Well, Sarah with an H! Tell me, what's your real name?"

"Sarah is my real name, but if you're asking about my legal name, it's Samuel."

"And, are you planning on legally getting your name changed to Sarah? Or is that just what everyone calls you?"

"Well, no... I mean, yes, my teachers, friends, and family refer to me as Sarah. But, you can't legally change your name in the system until eighteen. Same with surgery! I'm trapped in this body for another four years. But you're lucky though, being a senior and all, you don't have to wait much longer."

"Wait for what?" I asked in confusion.

"Surgery! You're trans, right?"

"No, honey! I'm not like you. I'm comfortable in my skin."

I continued touching up my make-up without even realizing what I had just said to Sarah. And then, I watched as his...her eyes quickly turned from a jolly green to pissed off dark brown!

"It's not about comfort. It is about knowing that you were

born into born in the wrong body and feeling like there's nothing you can do about it because society thinks something must be wrong with you. And, it's one thing to receive ignorance from people who aren't educated but getting it from people in your own community, that's a surprise!"

"Sarah, I didn't mean it like that..."

"It's just sad because I kind of looked up to you. I guess that's what I get for worshiping a false idol."

Sarah took one last look at me before making me taste the air as she quickly turned away and stormed out through the door. I immediately felt ashamed. It wasn't my intention to make her feel that way. But as I made my way out of the restroom and down the hall, I realized that maybe it was a defense mechanism to how I felt about myself. I was right when I said that I felt comfortable in my skin. I do and always have. But, I never strictly identified as one gender over the other. And I didn't know what that meant for me. Who was I if I didn't choose a side? I pondered that on my way to detention, where I met the rest of the gang. They were all sitting in the middle of the auditorium, except for Crystal. She was standing over Josh, yelling like a *Mad Mattress*, while Ms. Bailey stood outside the aisle, trying her best to defuse the situation.

"No, Josh. You're not listening. Jesuse has been living in his house for the past week without food. And now, he doesn't even have electricity! He needs help!" Crystal shouted.

"Crystal, we hear you! Unfortunately, we can only deal with one problem at a time, but I will talk to Principal Settle to make her aware of Jesuse's situation, see what we can do to help. It's been a long emotional couple of days for all of us. Just take a deep breath, and have a seat, please!"

I nervously smiled as I walked past Ms. Bailey while looking for an open seat next to Melanie and Gabrielle. They were sitting directly two rows down from Crystal and Josh. As I took my seat next to Melanie with Gabrielle sitting on the other side of her, I could immediately sense the tension brewing between them. We then waited for Crystal to finally flop down in her seat and hush so that Ms. Bailey could hand us our assignments dropped off by our teachers. Lord! Now, the first day of being in detention felt like an escape. But by the third day, I was missing the crowded classrooms and having lunch somewhere other than the tips of my knees. I was over it, honey, so over it! Then after Ms. Bailey handed us our assignments and ran to her office, the bickering between Melanie and Gabrielle began!

"Call me selfish, but I need to know...are we... together? What are we doing?" Melanie whispered to Gabrielle.

"I don't know. I mean, I thought we were... I'm just dealing with a lot at home on top of what's going on here. It's hard to think about a relationship right now." Gabrielle replied.

"Really, Gabrielle? *It's hard to think about a relationship?* Don't blame this on, on what happened Thursday night. You didn't have an issue holding my hand until your dad showed up. I mean, you ran out of the police station like you were afraid to be seen with me or something!"

"I'm sorry! What do you want me to say? I told you how my dad is... He doesn't even know that I'm...gay."

"Well, none of that seemed to matter to you before. So what did your dad say to you? He must have said something to get you to start acting like this."

"Like what? What am I doing?" Gabrielle asked.

"It's what you're not doing that's the problem."

As I continued to eavesdrop, so did my left shoulder onto Melanie's sweater. I was startled when Melanie shook me away, drawing attention to Gabrielle as they both paused and stared into my eyes. Melanie then said,

"Well, since you're so invested in the conversation, wanna help me understand this?"

"Sorry! I don't think I'm qualified to get involved in lesbian drama."

"Well, it looks to me like you've already gotten yourself involved..." Gabrielle replied.

"Fine, since you're both begging me for my input, but remember, I warned you. It sounds like you both are at two different places in whatever this relationship is. Melanie is out and proud, waving her rainbow flag of freedom, and Gabrielle, well, she needs help picking out her colors. And unfortunately, one of you will have to make a sacrifice to continue in your...whatever this is."

"Okay, stop saying it like that. It's a relationship! It's our relationship or the start of one. hell, I don't even know anymore." Melanie replied with vexation.

"Look, why don't you guys just forget I said anything!"

"No, I think you may have been spot on with most of what you said," Gabrielle replied.

"All I'm trying to say is... Okay, Gabrielle, if Melanie wanted you to introduce her to your dad, to proudly and loudly come out while holding her hand at the dinner table, would you?"

I waited for Gabrielle to reply, but the silence was all the proof I needed to be correct. Then I turned to Melanie and said,

"And Melanie, if Gabrielle wants you to live in secret, to hide your relationship from her family..."

"I'm not asking her to live in secret, just to give me time..." Gabrielle interrupted.

"And while she would be giving you time, you would be living in secret, no? Melanie, do you think you would be able to step back into the closet just to give Gabrielle more time?"

"I don't know..." Melanie softly replied as she glanced over at Gabrielle.

"Well, then it sounds to me like what you two have is a dilemma."

Well, it was true! I didn't feel any shame in telling them that, even though it resulted in me getting the side-eye and a couple of deep huffs and puffs. Honestly, I think love left a bitter taste in my mouth. The first boyfriend, the only boyfriend I ever had, died! No, he didn't die. Somebody killed him! I couldn't help feeling as though I was partly to blame. I turned my back on him when he needed me most. When James revealed the darkness within himself, I couldn't bear it. But what if that was my test? Or a twisted lesson for me to learn? What else was I supposed to do with his death? It couldn't have been for nothing. I thought, if I hadn't given up on James, maybe if I tried a little bit harder to understand him, we wouldn't have been in the woods arguing. Instead, we would have been on the dance floor, talking at least. After letting myself daydream the next thirty minutes away, we were all startled when out of nowhere, Principal Settle barged her way inside and rushed down the aisle towards us.

Ms. Bailey was still in her back office or wherever... And if you ask me, I think she was just hiding away so that she didn't have to deal with us and all of our drama. But Ms. Bailey had excellent timing because right when Principal Settle asked us where Ms. Bailey was, she appeared like magic from behind the curtain! The look of shock on her face was priceless, seeing Principal Settle staring back at her in confusion. Ms. Bailey then hurried her way downstage, and the two of them stood off in the distance, away from our prying ears, and began to whisper. Our noses widened as we anxiously waited for Ms. Bailey to spill the tea.

"What do you think they're talking about?" Gabrielle whispered.

"I don't know, honey! But whatever it is, it doesn't look good!" I whispered back.

Then after a few eye rolls our way from Principal Settle, she walked back out of the auditorium, leaving Ms. Bailey standing alone to deal with us. That's when I really started freaking out. Ms. Bailey then glared at us in dismay before she finally approached. And honey, the anticipation was killing me! I was dying to know what was going on. But just when I thought she was going to dish out a bunch of bad news, Ms. Bailey took a deep breath and said; *you're free to go!* But of course, we weren't free to go right at that moment. We had to wait until after first period. I was still baffled. I didn't know if the police had finally solved James's murder or what was going on! I had to find out. Minutes went by as I impatiently waited for the bell to ring. Once the bell finally sounded, I was off to see Principal Settle. I darted out of the auditorium so fast that I tripped over my shoe!

When I finally made it to the principal's office, out of breath and sweating like a hog, the secretary told me to have a seat and that Principal Settle would be out in a few minutes. So I did just that. After taking a seat, I heard the one voice I never thought I'd hear, screaming in agony. Though the door was closed, I could still hear every word.

"My son has been dead for almost a week, six days to be exact! And you're not doing a damn thing to help bring my family justice! Instead, you let these kids parade around here as if nothing happened. My son's murderer is here, in the walls of this school. So if you refuse to do your job by finding the person responsible, I'll do it myself!"

Seconds later, I heard the door swing open as it loudly slammed against the wall. It was Mrs. Bernard. I could see her tears running the eyeliner down her cheeks. And then she looked at me. It felt like time had frozen. As if Mrs. Bernard could see into my soul. I didn't know if I had the right to ask about the funeral or even speak to her. But as she quickly buttoned up her blue pea coat, I stood up and calmly approached.

"Mrs. Bernard, words can't describe how sorry I am. James, he didn't deserve any of this! Neither does your family. I want you to know how much I miss James and how sorry I am..."

"Sorry for what, Toni?" Mrs. Bernard asked as she finished buttoning her coat.

I tried to keep it together. I tried not to burst out into tears right in front of her, but I felt it coming. I was speechless, and then Mrs. Bernard went on to say,

"Toni, you have nothing to be sorry for, you loved my son, and he loved you. I don't know what went on in your relationship, but I at least know that much. And listen, uh, we're having a wake for James this Saturday, at 1:30 P.M. It'll be at our house. I hope you'll be there. And if you heard what I just said in there, know that I'm just a brokenhearted mother, looking for the truth. So, if you know anything, I don't care how upset you think that it'll make me, please…tell me."

"I promise, Mrs. Bernard, I will tell you as soon as I know something."

Mrs. Bernard then smiled as she wiped her tears and patted me on the shoulder. I watched as she slowly walked out of the room, and immediately, I felt ashamed. I was embarrassed because she didn't know how I really felt about James. It took Principal Settle startling me from behind to shake me out of my daze. And after speaking to Mrs. Bernard, I had forgotten what I was doing in the principal's office in the first place. With seconds left, I rushed to class and stopped by my locker on the way. I just kept thinking about James and his mother and the conversation I had with her about how she believed that James and I loved each other. *Did he really love me?* I honestly couldn't tell. As I've mentioned before, there were good moments between us, moments where I felt like the luckiest person on the planet. But the moments that weren't, the times where James made me feel smaller than the nucleus of a cell, those moments were unbearable.

And I'd often wrestle with myself, wondering how I could feel an ounce of sympathy for someone who inflected over a ton of pain onto me, mentally and physically. Then I'd tell myself not to judge. That the pain James was harboring inside had nothing to do with me, but instead, everything to do with himself. And then I'd imagine a world where James didn't face abuse, where he still had some of his innocence left. I imagined that this James would have grown into a kind, compassionate, empathetic young man. I also believed that I got a tiny taste of what that James could have been like if his life turned out differently. But what troubled most was replaying the conversation we had in the woods moments before it happened. It's heavy, knowing you could have possibly played a part in someone else's demise. I may not have been able to carry on a relationship with James, but maybe I could have been his friend. Oh, but what am I thinking? James would have never settled for less than what he wanted.

Most times, it isn't the person we are battling but rather the battles inside that particular person. I learned that we humans, these balls of energies roaming around as vessels, have so much power, more power than we realize over each other. We can even alter each other's energies, and whether positive or negative, the effects could transcend lifetimes. But if we can have this much power over each other, I wonder what would happen if we realized how much power we have over ourselves? It sort of reminds me of the conversation I had with Sarah earlier in the morning. I didn't know at the time that my inability to understand Sarah could have a lasting effect on who she chooses to open up to in the future. But I was hopeful that Sarah wouldn't hold a grudge. On my way to lunch, I met up with Gabrielle, and we had a chance to talk more freely without being smothered by Crystal and Josh.

Right as I sat down, Gabrielle just smiled. She always had a smile on her face. Even when she wasn't happy, she still had a way of making others feel warm inside. So, I smiled back, returning the positive energy, and I said,

"Oh my God! I'm so happy to see you outside of that auditorium. No offense Gabrielle, but if I had to spend another day in there, with Crystal and Josh, I was going to pull out the magic pen and join James in the afterlife."

"Oh, don't joke like that, Toni! But I understand. Even I have my limits when it comes to sharing the stage. If I can't sing or perform, I don't see the need to be in the auditorium," Gabrielle chuckled.

"You're a mess! But seriously, how have you been dealing with everything? I was interviewed three different times by the police."

"Wow? They only talked to me once, that night. I guess the police have their minds made up already of who they believe is more likely to be guilty or not."

"What do you mean?" I asked.

"I'm just saying; I heard Crystal saying something similar, that the police barely spoke to her."

"Oh my God, honey! They don't seriously think it's me, do they?"

"I don't know...but don't worry, I think Josh got that taken care of for you."

Before I could even ask what Gabrielle meant by, *Josh took care of that for me*; Melanie sat down, right next to Gabrielle, and blurted out,

"Took care of what?"

"Well, Hey, honey! Don't you just love being back inside a real cafeteria? Oh and, where's Renee? I haven't seen her all week," I asked.

"That's because we've been sitting in detention! But Renee's not here today. She's playing hooky, which is what we all should be doing. Anyway, what are you guys talking about?" Melanie asked.

"We were talking about how Josh got Biscuit in trouble with the police. He's now a suspect. And come to think of it, I haven't seen Biscuit around today. Do you guys think he really did it? Maybe that's why we're free?" Gabrielle said.

"It's possible. But, it doesn't make any sense. None of this does. Yes, Biscuit is a neo nazi, trailer park, Ku klutz klan member birthed from hell. But why would he kill James?" Melanie asked.

"Because he's also a neo nazi homophobic, all of the above, birthed from hell," I replied.

"True! But Biscuit's not sloppy. He doesn't seem like the type who would get his own hands dirty. I mean, have you ever seen him get into a fight? Homophobic or not, there would be no logical reason for Biscuit to kill James," Melanie replied.

I then glanced over in Josh's direction, where he was sitting with a couple of the guys on the football team. They were sitting a few tables away, more towards the center of the cafeteria, and I could just feel him watching me. It spooked the hell out of me. I couldn't understand why he was glaring in our direction, and then it hit me,

"Unless we don't have all the pieces of the puzzle, I wouldn't be so quick to put it into the realm of impossibility."

As we continued with our lunch, I saw Sarah, with an H, approaching. I immediately wanted to shrivel up in my chair and hide, but instead, I smiled and waved. Sarah only continued walking, giving me enough shade to keep me cool for the rest of the day! Melanie and Gabrielle noticed, which did not help at all!

"Well, what the heck, Toni! What did you do to Sarah?" Melanie asked.

"I didn't do anything…"

"I don't know, from the looks of it, I'd say that you made your first enemy. I'm proud of you! The way I see it, one hasn't truly lived until they've made a few enemies!"

"I didn't do anything, okay! I just might have said something without thinking. And how do you guys know Sarah anyway?"

"Toni, everyone knows Sarah. She's the first trans person we have had at this school, ever! I think she's pretty brave!" Gabrielle replied.

"See, I can't do that as naturally as you," I added.

"Do what?" Gabrielle asked.

"It's hard for me to call someone who has an Adam's apple bigger than mine and a voice box deeper than Berry White's, a… she. And I know, I know it sounds horrible. But I'm just being honest. I'm not against what Sarah is doing; I'm rooting for Sarah and all of us to live in a world where we can be whoever the hell we want to be. Correction! Where we can be whoever the hell, we were born to be, without trepidation."

"Sarah's voice is not deeper than Berry White's. I don't think anyone can go deeper than that!" Melanie chucked as she tried and failed to reenact, *Practice What You Preach.*

"Don't listen to Melanie. She's trying to be a comedian. Listen to me, Toni...We have been conditioned to think, right vs. wrong, up vs. down, male or female for so many years. You're in one box or the other. And if you don't fit into a recognizable box, you are marked unidentified. It's not about what you see physically; it's about what you feel. Scientists have categorized us as being female without a penis, and male without..."

"Don't forget about the hermaphrodites...." Melanie interrupted.

"Yes, that word! I mean, they couldn't come up with a better word to describe being born with both male and female parts? It's like straight vs. gay. But only one of those sounds correct. Anyway, I won't get into that because we'd be sitting here for the rest of the day. My point is that you are what you feel, and no scientist or doctor should confine you to a box that makes scientific sense. It's easy for me to call Sarah, she, because I'm not looking at her physical make-up. I'm looking at her soul. Men are Kings while women are Queens. You know that only one sounds more dominant than the other, yet women have and always will be the brains of the majority of operations for centuries and centuries to come...

"Sorry, Toni! But, why aren't women called, Kings? I'll tell you why? It's because we've all been brainwashed to live in a Black and White society for generations. We are going to have to be the ones who start the reprogramming process. And lastly, but most importantly, it's out of respect! Respect and believe who people tell you they are."

Wow! Gabrielle completely blew my mind. I was surprised that she had that much passion inside her, especially for someone still hiding in the closet. But I gave my girl her props while also taking mental notes. So as we continued our chat, I suddenly noticed out the corner of my eye a woman staring at me through the cafeteria glass window. The poor thing was dressed in a hideous thick black coat and wore box braids from the 90s. The woman just about gave me a heart attack as she waved my way anxiously. I almost couldn't tell if I was hallucinating this woman or if she was one of our classmates playing a senior prank. Either way, I had to get to the bottom of it.

"Guys, don't look, but... a creepy-ass old woman is standing outside waving at us through the window."

And what did they do? They both looked, no gawked, like owls.

"I told you guys not to look!"

"Oh my God," Melanie replied as she held her head down.

"What is it? Do you know who that is?"

"Yes, unfortunately, I do. That creepy ass old woman is my mother."

The woman just continued waving, trying to get Melanie's attention. And though many students were eating outside, I was surprised that nobody noticed this strange lady walking on school property, not to mention the security. I mean, where were they? Finally, Melanie wiped the food off her mouth, took her tray, and got up from the table. Gabrielle and I watched as Melanie headed out of the cafeteria to greet her mother.

"What do you think she wants with Melanie?" Gabrielle asked.

"I don't know…but what I do know is that Melanie clearly got her looks from her dad."

"Seriously?" Gabrielle snarled.

"Sorry, I just couldn't help but notice. So, what's going on with you guys anyway? I mean, before we became *America's Most Wanted*, you two were like Ruth and Naomi, the untold story. I hope you're not going to let your dad get in the way of your happiness…"

"I know… it's just; this is all new to me. Now that it's real and no longer a fantasy in my head, there's more pressure. Pressure for me to come out, and I can't do that right now, not alone. It's much easier when you have parents who understand, but all I have is a dad who sees the world behind uncolored lenses. And Melanie doesn't deserve someone who would ask her to hide who she is. I don't want to do that to her."

"Then don't! I know that it's not easy, and my parents weren't always accepting like they are now. But how are we going to make a change? How are we even going to begin the reprogramming process if we are still stuck ourselves?"

I let Gabrielle ponder that thought as I looked out the window to see what Melanie was doing. But as I looked, Melanie was nowhere to be found. I stood up and looked through the glass outside as far as I could see, but there was no Melanie or strange mother in sight. I panicked!

"Gabrielle, do you see Melanie?"

Gabrielle stood up to look out the window with me, then I asked,

"Remind me, didn't her mother try to kill her like five years ago or something like that?"

"Uh...y-yeah... What if, and I hate to think this but, what if that bullet wasn't meant for James after all?"

"Shit! We need to tell someone, uhm, Principal Settle!" I replied.

Gabrielle and I flew right out of the cafeteria and headed straight to the principal's office. I felt like an idiot for not piecing it all together sooner. With everything that's been going on, James's death had become the center of my universe. I hoped and prayed that I wouldn't be on the verge of losing one of the most incredible friends I've come to know. Having to deal with one death was tragic enough, but two, my mind couldn't fathom the thought. After Gabrielle and I made it to the office and begged the secretary to let us talk to Principal Settle, she told us to have a seat. We were itching for Principal Settle to come out of her office; we were running out of time. Every minute we spent sitting, not looking for Melanie, was another minute wasted. When Principal Settled finally emerged from her cave, we cried out to her,

"Please, we need your help. You need to call the police. Melanie is gone!"

"Wait, slow down. What are you talking about?" Principal Settled asked.

"Her mom was here, standing outside of the cafeteria staring at us. We didn't think much of it at the time, but now Melanie is gone! We think she left with her!" Gabrielle shouted.

"Okay, Gabrielle, relax. I'm sure Melanie didn't go far. You still have twenty minutes left in the lunch period. Where exactly did you two last see Melanie?"

Before we could answer Principal Settle's question, out of nowhere, we heard the softest voice say in the angriest of tones,

"Excuse me! What did you just say?"

And there she was, Ms. Bloom. She startled the three of us as we each looked up and glared her way. Ms. Bloom then walked closer to Gabrielle and me with her arms folded, demanding answers.

"Did I just hear you say that Melanie is missing because you two weren't competent enough to tell a teacher, faculty, or ANYBODY that a stranger was on school property, until now?"

"Why don't we calm down, Jennifer. There's no need to get upset!" Principal Settle replied.

"And there's also no need for you to speak to me like a child! I've been telling you for months that this school needs better security. Anyone can just walk on and off the property at any time without being seen. The security you hired is a joke! If this school had better protection, we wouldn't be in this situation, burying one of our own. Now, I'm telling you, that woman is not to be trusted! She tried to kill her own daughter, for God's sake. She should not be allowed on school property, ever!

Ms. Bloom then turned back to Gabrielle and me while staring us deep in the eyes and added,

"If anything happens to Melanie… it'll be on the two of you!"

Ms. Bloom gave us one last cold stare before storming out of the room. Immediately, I broke down. It was too much to handle. I felt stupid for not paying more attention, for not even thinking to follow Melanie when she walked outside. Principal Settle informed us that she would look around herself to see if she could find Melanie and reminded both Gabrielle and me not to worry. After that, all I could do was bunch up my feelings and walk out of the office in tears.

"Toni! Toni, wait! I'm sure that Melanie's okay!" Gabrielle said.

"She's not okay! You don't just leave your best friend alone with the one person who once tried to kill her."

"Well, how do you think I feel, huh? I'm supposed to be her girlfriend, or, well, I don't even know at this point what we are. But it doesn't mean that I love her any less. It doesn't mean that you care any less. I mean, what were we supposed to do? Go out there and be her bodyguards? Melanie's mom just got out of prison. So I'm betting that all she wanted to do was talk."

Talk! Even I knew better. Gabrielle was sweet for trying to help, but I felt like I needed to do something other than having faith. As we headed back to the cafeteria, I began thinking that maybe I was just overreacting. I talked myself into believing that once we walked through those cafeteria doors, Melanie would be sitting at the table, dazed and confused, throwing her hands up in the air, wondering where we had gone. But instead, when Gabrielle and I returned, the table where I hoped Melanie would be sitting was empty. Gabrielle and I then took one look at each other before heading outside. Principal Settled soon joined us in our search along with Ms. Bailey and Ms. Bloom.

It felt like we were on one of those CSI shows doing our own missing person's search. When lunch was over, and everyone began heading back to their classes, it became clearer that Melanie was no longer at school. Gabrielle and I swapped numbers so that in case whichever one of us found Melanie, first, we could notify the other. I spent the rest of the day in each of my classes checking my phone constantly. I waited hour by hour, minute-by-minute, and my heart sunk knowing that by the end of the day, Melanie still had not returned. Right then, when the last bell sounded, releasing us to go home, is when a terrifying thought occurred to me. I thought if Melanie's mom could walk on school and stand right outside the cafeteria unnoticed in broad daylight, then what would stop a total stranger from sneaking up on us in the dark?

| 5 |

MELANIE

THE TIME was 6:55 P.M., precisely as I looked up at the giant digital clock in front of bank, the only real light I had. I was lost, in the middle of nowhere, in almost complete darkness. I found myself walking alongside the road with fewer cars than there was just an hour before sunset, and I was freezing my ass off in the cold. Now, remember, this was December. And winter in the state of Indiana is real. The temperature had dropped down to 36 degrees, and all I had with me was my blue jean jacket and red beanie to keep me warm. I left my coat in my locker along with my other belongings after being bullied into cutting class by my lunatic mother. Now, how did I end up miles away from home, stranded in the middle of nowhere on a school night? I'll have to rewind the clock for about nine hours to explain how I ended up in such a predicament.

I was having lunch with Toni and Gabrielle at around 11 A.M. The last thing I remember them talking about before my mother showed up to the school dressed like Darth Vader was the misconception of trans people. Gabrielle and I were also trying to work through our relationship or decide, better yet, if we even still had one. In my mind, I thought that we did, especially after that kiss. But, I didn't understand what changed or why she let fear run her in the opposite direction. Gabrielle wanted me; she pretty much begged me to be with her. Then once she had me, once I placed my heart directly into the palm of her hand, she decided it was too heavy to carry. I understood to a certain extent the pressure Gabrielle was under with coming out to her dad, especially being an only child. But, I couldn't understand why she changed with me.

But even so, I was pretty impressed with how Gabrielle handled herself as she preached about the power of respect and transgender pronouns. I was smiling inside and out just from thinking how lucky I was to be in the presence of someone so open-minded and humble. Then, Toni completely changed the mood by saying,

"Guys, don't look, but… a creepy-ass homeless woman is standing outside waving at us through the window."

I don't know how but I knew it without looking. I could feel this numbness in the pit of my stomach, this inner voice telling me that it was her. And as I turned my head to the left of me, my gut proved me correct. My mother was staring back at me, dressed in a black leather trench coat with a hat to match.

"I told you guys not to look!" Toni whispered.

After informing Toni and Gabrielle that the creepy woman staring back at us was, in fact, my mother, I went outside to confront her. I didn't understand what she was doing showing up to my school in the middle of the day. I planned to shoo her away. However, the conversation took an unexpected turn.

"What…what are you doing here? You're not supposed to be here!" I asked in a low tone.

Worried about the attention we'd draw, I walked my mother to the side of the building, where we were mostly out of sight.

"In case you forgot, I'm your mother, not Ms. Bailey. I've been trying to contact you all week, but you've been refusing to take my calls. So, I came to the only place that I knew you couldn't hide."

"What do you want?" I barked.

"Don't talk to me like that! I'm here because I wanted to see you. And, I need your help."

"Of course you do…"

"You know, all those years you spent living with that teacher sure has made you a smart ass. But I'm back now, and I'll fix that!"

"I don't need to listen to this; I'm going back inside…."

As I started to walk away, my mother yanked me by the arm and said,

"Don't be stupid, and test me, Melanie. All I have to do is walk through those doors and tell your principal that one of her teachers is having an inappropriate relationship with her student. And that Ms. Bloom of yours will be on her way to the state penitentiary. Now, you can walk away, or you can help me!"

After yanking my arm back, I replied,

"If you were going to say something about that, you would have done it already. But whatever Ms. Bloom said to you while you were locked up, I know it got you scared. So what does she know about you? I mean, besides the obvious?"

Standing by the side of the building, listening to chatter from the distance, I waited for my mother to reply; instead, she just looked away in shame. I quickly became fed up and started to walk away again. Though the second time around, my mother decided she'd put on her begging shoes."

"Wait! Please! I really do need your help. I have a couple of job interviews today, and I don't have a car to get around!"

"Well, neither do I. And if you need to get around, there's something called a taxi! I'm sure they can help you out."

"I don't have enough time to wait around for a cab. I need a car! And with my license now expired, look, I know that woman helped you get your license. So just help me out!"

"I'm not even old enough to rent a car."

"That's okay. I got a friend in town that I used to rent from regularly. He says he can help us out."

"You're always begging me to do things for you...but when are you ever going to start doing things for me, other than making my life a living hell? You don't even feel an ounce of regret for the pain you've caused. You haven't changed. Why should I even consider helping you?"

"You're right, Melanie. I'm trying to do better. God gave me a second chance, a fresh start! And I'm asking you one last time for your help."

I knew I should have walked away. I wanted to hit her where it would hurt the most, tell her how horrible of a mother she was. But instead, I ended up falling for the lines as I followed her off school property and down the street. I had gotten so used to being unnoticed by my mother that I took what she said as an apology. Pathetic, I know! I was desperate for whatever would come close. We then continued walking down the street to the nearest bus stop. After waiting 10 minutes, a bus pulled up, and we got on and rode for about 30 minutes. We were then dropped off right in front of Bennies Car Rental shop. Once inside, I had to listen to her play catch-up with the owner for about 45 minutes. Afterward, we were finally ready to hit the road in a rented, black 2009 Chevy Impala. I was nervous, you know, being alone with her again, in a car! I had no idea what my mother had up her sleeve. I was driving for not even five minutes before my mother told me that she wanted to take over.

"Melanie, I want you to stop at this gas station up ahead so we can get out and switch."

"What? We can't do that! Your license is expired, remember?"

"Even with an expired license, I can drive better than you. You drive slower than a turtle. Now, go ahead and pull over right there!"

The feeling I had in my stomach earlier, the nausea, well, it had twice doubled at that point. At least with me driving, I felt somewhat in control. As I said, I didn't feel good about being alone with my mother, and then the idea of letting her take control of the wheel was terrifying. So after she stared me down for what felt like ten minutes, we got out and switched. My mother was fully in charge, and my life, yet again, was at the mercy of her hands. She could tell that I slowly lost my confidence, that I grew back into my thirteen-year-old self again. My heart rate increased as we drove onto the highway, leaving what has become my safe place. At that point, I didn't understand what we were doing or where we were headed. But, I tried to play it cool by asking,

"How many interviews do you have?"

"Just a couple…"

"Where?" I barked.

"Why, Melanie? You know, you seem a little nervous. Not so tough anymore now that you don't have your teachers around to coddle you, huh? Don't worry. I'm not going to hurt you. I just wanted to spend time with my one and only daughter. Is that okay?"

I didn't know how to respond after that. I suddenly remembered the etiquette my mother taught me as a child. You know, when to speak, when not to speak, etc. I only had one last question as we came upon the city limits sign. I looked at her face, covered in sickness masked by an occasional smile, and I asked,

"Where are we going?"

"It's a surprise… we're almost there."

A surprise? I knew that with her, nothing good ever came from the word. Her kind of surprise almost ended my life. I just hoped that she wasn't trying to take me out of the state. Although, if she were, maybe that would benefit me in the long run, seeing as she was on probation and not allowed to cross the border. After another 20 minutes of driving through flat farmland, we ended up in Cedar Lake at an old country home. This house sat right on the water, surrounded by lots of greenery. I was confused; I didn't understand what she was doing. Then after my mom parked, she quickly jumped out of the car and hollered for me to follow behind. I slowly got out and followed her instructions, but secretly, I was trying to figure out my escape.

As we made our way to the front porch, an older gentleman came out to greet us. I had never seen this man before. I just ogled back and forth between the two of them as they both smiled at one another and then broke into tears. It was such an awkward moment for me as I just stood there emotionless and puzzled. When the man began embracing my mother, I couldn't help but judge his clothing. The gentleman was wearing these warn out blue overalls and a white V-neck t-shirt. He even had a scruffy silver beard. After an extended emotional greeting, my mother finally introduced me.

"This is Melanie, my daughter...Melanie, this is your grandpa, Lewis."

What the hell he was! I'd never seen that man a day in my life. And now, after 18 years, she wanted to introduce me to him as her daughter. Ha! I almost cracked up over that one. I assumed that he wasn't familiar with the daily press; otherwise, he'd be turning her away instead of welcoming the two of us inside. I took a look around, and I will admit that he had a beautiful home, once you were on the inside at least. Everything had a wood polish to it. The floors, the stairs, even parts of the walls had a wooden touch. As we made our way inside the kitchen and took our seats at the table, I wondered if I would be greeted by mama Berenstain next. But it appeared that Mr. Lewis, or whoever he was, lived alone. After asking me loads of questions that I didn't have the answers to, he offered my mother and me a cup of tea. While he continued to talk to us from the stove, I whispered to her,

"What are we doing here? I thought you said you had an interview?"

"Well, this is it! Now, don't be rude. Your grandpa is asking you a question."

It made my insides fume when she'd refer to Mr. Lewis as my grandpa. But, I knew how to be polite and polite I was,

"I apologize, Mr. Lewis, I didn't hear you. Could you repeat the question?"

"Don't worry about it, sweetie. I was just asking about your plans after high school! Do you have a college in mind?"

"No, I'm not sure. I play softball, but I don't think I'm good enough to go pro. I haven't thought about what I wanted to do after high school. I just hope to be alive long enough to figure it out," I replied while glaring over at my mother.

Yes, you are correct. That was a dig! And she quickly caught on to my remark as she gave me the ultimate mother death stare. I then asked to be excused to use the restroom. After checking the time from the clock on the wall, 2:30 P.M. it read. I got the idea to give Ms. Bailey a call to let her know where I was if anything was to, God forbid, happen to me again. After being dismissed from the table, I hurried to the restroom and immediately reached for my phone. But of course, it was dead, and my charger was in my backpack at school. I was completely and utterly screwed in the middle of nowhere Cedar Lake country with two strangers. So, I stalled, tried to think of a plan, a way to escape, but with Mr. Lewis's bathroom window being the size of a small doggie door, I began to run out of solutions. And before I could flush the toilet, pretending I had used it, my mother opened the door and invited herself inside.

"What are you..."

I couldn't even finish my sentence. My mother had grabbed me by the face with her right hand and dug her nails so deeply into my cheeks that I couldn't even move my mouth. She then went on to say,

"I don't know what the hell your problem is, but if you embarrass me like that again in front of my daddy, I'll give you a real reason to be afraid."

Then after yanking my face back and almost giving me whiplash, she just stared at me. We stood face-to-face, well, more like forehead to chin. My mother was a couple of inches taller, bigger, and more robust. Even as an adult, she had a way of making me feel small. I just continue to stare at her in disgust and said,

"I don't belong here. I'm leaving! So go ahead, do whatever you think you need to do to scare me. I survived death once before; I'll survive it again."

I started to walk out of the bathroom, and then my mother hit me with,

"I'm taking you out of that bitch's house, and you're going to live here with your grandpa Lewis! You will help him out around the house, the yard, and you'll take care of him when you're not in school. It's time that you get to know your family."

"Why? It's not like you care about me. I'm just a free, life-size punching bag to you. And about family, I already have that, and I've gotten to know my family pretty well."

"Who? Your teachers? That Ms. Bailey don't give a damn about you! You say that I'm just using you to be my punching bag? Hm, well, let me tell you something, Melanie. That woman only sees you as a check! There's not one person in this world that's not existing, living, and breathing for themselves, and only for themselves. You need to wake up from the fairytale sleeping beauty and step into the real world. People are not who you think they are. In a world filled with fairytale love, you'll soon find out how replaceable you really are!"

"Give me the keys... I'll drive myself back to town!"

"Really? And how are you going to do that? You don't even know how to get back! No! The only thing you're going to do is walk your ass back into that kitchen, sit down at the table, and enjoy the cup of tea grandpa Lewis just made for you."

"Fine... If you won't give me the keys, I'll walk back!"

As I tried to shove my way through, my mother grabbed my beanie, catching my hair along with it, and pushed me to the ground. Immediately, Mr. Lewis came rushing to the door and shouted,

"Is everything okay?"

"Yes! We're fine, daddy! You know how tiny this bathroom is. We'll be out in a minute!"

"Alright..."

I listened as the foot steps fade away with every creek. Still sitting on the floor, staring up at my unapologetic mother, I said,

"You won't be happy until I'm dead, will you? Is this what, *trying to change, looks like?*"

I slowly stood up, grabbed my beanie from the floor, and

put it back on my head. I then took a step closer, staring intensely into my mother's eyes, and spoke once more.

"You keep putting your hands on me, and eventually, I stop being afraid. Eventually, I'll start fighting back."

I left my mother with that thought as I slowly walked past her and through the bathroom door. Out of respect because I took pride in being mannerly, I said goodbye to Mr. Lewis on my way out. He followed me into the living room with such disappointment in his eyes and asked,

"Well, where are you going? I just met you, and you're leaving already?"

"Things aren't what they appear to be, Mr. Lewis. I think you should spend this time getting to know your daughter. But uh, thanks for the tea. Maybe I can come by one day and actually enjoy it with you."

I walked out of the front door and stood there, staring ahead at the tall trees. I had no idea what I was going to do or how I would get back home. I eventually found myself walking through the woods behind Mr. Lewis's house. I was still in shock from the events that happened, but I was more concerned with the possibility of my mother following me. So I decided to hide near one of the tree stumps that sat next to a small hill. I needed a moment to clear my mind. Also, I needed to figure out how the hell I was going to get back home. I didn't care about the rental or what my beast of a mother planned on doing with it. I couldn't think about that. All I knew was that I would soon be losing sunlight and only had ten dollars in my wallet.

After waiting about 45 minutes to make sure that I was clear to keep walking, I hiked until I found the nearest road.

And that road led me to a small diner. It was almost 4:00 P.M. when I walked inside asking for directions. I was starving! So, I decided to buy something off the menu before I continued on my journey. The waitress brought me a glass of water, a cup of hot chocolate, and a map. While I waited for them to cook my burger, I tried my best to study the directions. Unfortunately, when you grow up in a generation that uses Google maps for everything, one quickly finds that navigating an actual map is almost like learning a foreign language. I had no idea what was north or south. My patience started to wither away like the whipped cream in my hot chocolate. I sadly considered walking back to Mr. Lewis's house and calling it a night. I'm sure that's what my mother was hoping I'd do. But I wasn't going to give her the satisfaction of having me show up on their doorstep, begging to come back inside.

So, after another hour, I decided to follow the map as best as I could, and I began my hike back to town. I made sure to ask for the time before leaving. It was precisely 5:10 P.M. when I started my walk. I knew it would be dangerous to be out alone, correction, dangerous to be a female walking alone in the dark, so I stayed close to as many buildings as possible. I watched as the last glimmer of sunlight faded away, and the trees turned from dark green to black. After walking for an hour and forty-five minutes, I had to take a break. It was ice cold, and my feet were killing me! I found myself near a bus stop, and I took a seat on the bench. What was supposed to be a five-minute rest break turned into an hour's nap. By the time I woke up, I was grateful that my body had remained untouched and that my shoes and clothes were still intact. I asked around once more for directions, and surely enough, I was just an hour away from town. I started getting excited! I got my blood flowing, and I was ready to complete the marathon. I pushed myself to keep walking minute by minute and block-by-block until 40 minutes passed and I was back into town.

I realized that I only had about fifty cents left in my pocket, so I searched for the nearest bus stop. After walking another 15 minutes, I came to a bus stop and saw the bus pulling up right in front of me. When the bus stopped and the doors opened, I begged the driver to let me on with just fifty cents. I guess he was in a good mood that night because I got on the bus and kept my fifty cents too! I then found a seat towards the front, flopped down, and took a deep celebratory breath. My feet felt stiff, and my heels were on fire! When I finally arrived back in my neighborhood, I became more anxious by the second at the thought of rinsing away the dirt that piled up on my skin and cozying up in my warm bed. When I finally made it to Ms. Bailey's house and found myself standing in front of that big blue door, I didn't even have to knock. Ms. Bailey opened the door for me.

"Melanie! Melanie, is that you?"

Ms. Bailey gave me the biggest welcome home hug ever. She must have squeezed me for five minutes straight because I didn't even notice the person who stood right behind her.

"Melanie, where did you go? Everybody was so worried! Are you okay?"

She did a scan of my face and body as she patted me down, checking to see that I was okay. I just smiled, out of breath, and said,

"It's okay. I'm okay! I'm just happy to be back home."

"Well, were you with your mom?"

Before I could reply, I glanced over Ms. Bailey's shoulder and became flabbergasted when I could clearly see the person staring back at me with a crooked smile. I then asked,

"What's going on? What's this?"

"Oh, Jesuse is going to stay here for a while. Just until he can get on his feet."

Jesuse was standing right over Ms. Bailey's shoulder, pretending to care, dressed in his pajamas. He didn't know what to say at first. He only stared with worrying eyes. I knew that he was grieving the loss of his mother, but I sadly didn't care. I was too focused on my own feelings to think to ask if he was okay. I remember thinking that maybe my mother was right about Ms. Bailey.

"I was gone for not even 24 hours, and you replaced me that fast?"

"Melanie, Jesuse has been through more than you can imagine. I couldn't sit by and just do nothing. I have an extra room, and as I said, it's just until he gets on his feet."

There was an awkward silence as I stepped into the room, that was until Jesuse said,

"I don't want to cause any problems, Ms. Bailey. I should probably go…"

"No! You're not going anywhere. I didn't spend two and a half hours convincing you to come here, just for you to turn around and go back home. You're staying. I'm more than happy to have you stay."

"Great! Then it looks like I'll be the one leaving!" I angrily replied.

I brushed my way past Ms. Bailey and Jesuse and headed

to my room to grab a change of clothes and the spare phone charger I kept plugged into the wall socket. As I started packing, Ms. Bailey calmly walked inside as she tried to convince me to stay.

"Melanie, you don't have to leave! I don't want you to leave. There's plenty of room here for the both of you. I'm sure you two will barely see each other anyway. You have the entire attic to yourself! Jesuse won't be a bother. I can tell that you've had a rough day. You need to get some rest!"

"Rough? Rough would be too generous of a word to describe the day that I had."

It didn't take me long to pack an outfit, a few hygiene products, and my phone charger. Finally, I was ready to go before Ms. Bailey began her next thought.

"Melanie, stop for a minute and hear me out!"

I stopped and stood in front of the doorway, waiting to hear what Ms. Bailey had to say.

"Jesuse just lost his mother. And his living conditions, he was living in a house without food and power. You know my heart. I couldn't let him live like that or become a part of the system, especially with the holidays right around the corner."

"I understand that…I do. What I don't understand is why you didn't look for me? While my mom was playing, *Whack-A-Mole* with my head, you were here having pizzas with Jesuse. Did you even try looking for me or calling? Or did you just assume that I was okay?"

"That's not fair, Melanie. I did try to call you, but your phone kept going to voicemail. I didn't want to panic until I had a reason to. I didn't think that if you were with your mother, that you would be in any real danger, but I was concerned, very!"

"How could you not think I would be in any danger? I thought I was special, important to you because you loved me. But it had nothing to do with love at all. It's just who you are. Helping others makes you feel good. But, I have one question: if we are taking care of everyone else and they are also taking care of each other, then who's taking care of us? Who's looking out for us, for me?"

Ms. Bailey was speechless. I could read the disappointment all over her face. I wish I had been more understanding, more grateful for all that she's done. But, instead, I couldn't help feeling forgotten, betrayed. It felt like African Americans, people of color, or whichever term you prefer to use, have been stuck for centuries, trying to climb out of fast-sinking quicksand. I thought that we as a people were finally starting to get it right by taking care of each other and put each other first. But after leaving Ms. Bailey alone in my room and running into Jesue at the foot of the stairs, I was reminded that when you live in a world filled with fairytale love, one can easily be replaced!

| 6 |

GABRIELLE

THURSDAY, oh dear! Thursday has become another word added to my superstitious list. After walking down the hall wearing my yellow skirt and matching socks, I was hopeful that the day wouldn't end in murder like the week before. I was so ready for Christmas break. I loved seeing the little decorations, lights, candy canes, presents, and even my homie Santa. Yeah, I knew I was too old to be a fan, but why do we have to stop believing in magic just because our age outgrows our height? Through all the darkness and despair, I could still see the light. And at seventeen, your girl Gabrielle still believed he was somewhere out there Ho Ho-ing on a sled. I mean, come on, where did they get the idea from anyway? Those were the outrageous pep talks I had to give myself to keep from going insane! But I remember this day well. I was at my locker getting my books together for my first-period class, and I overheard Melanie and Renee talking as they approached.

"Thanks again for letting me crash last night. And for also

letting me vent your ear off. It seems like you're the only person I can count on these days."

"Girl, anytime! We're family. Mi casa es su casa!" Renee replied.

I was ecstatic that Melanie was okay and back in school, considering the events that took place the day before. I hadn't even heard from Melanie until I saw her walking with Renee. And before I let Melanie walk past me, I shouted,

"Melanie! Were you really going to walk by and not say anything? I've been worried about you!"

"Hey, sorry, I didn't see you. I'm okay. My feet are still sore, and my back feels like crap but, I think in a few hours, I'll be back to normal," Melanie replied.

"I'm so sorry about yesterday. Toni and I, we never should have let walk outside alone."

"Why? It's not your responsibility to take care of me. I'm a big girl."

While the three of us continued chatting by my locker, I was shockingly distracted when Ms. Bloom approached with all of her dramatics as she glared at Melanie and said,

"Jesus, Melanie? What happened to you? Where have you been? Are you okay?"

Ms. Bloom shoved Renee and me out of the way as she ran up towards Melanie, expressing a little too much concern if you ask me. Melanie then said,

"Yes... I'm okay, just a little exhausted, but I'm good."

"Are you sure? Did she hurt you?"

Ms. Bloom then started to rub Melanie's shoulders. Ugh, the nerve of her. I just stood there with my arms folded, waiting for the woman to acknowledge that she rudely shoved her way in front of me. After Melanie reassured Ms. Bloom that she was okay for the fifth time, she went on to say,

"Okay! Well, I want you to know that my door is always open if you need anything, anything at all. And I mean it."

Ugh, seriously? My door is always open? Please! As if Renee and I weren't smart enough to figure that one out. I couldn't take any more of her mushy vibes. I was growing furious by the second. So I loudly cleared my throat and said,

"EXCUSE ME!"

Ms. Bloom quickly turned around and pretended like she didn't notice I was hovering centimeters behind her.

"Oh, Gabrielle! I'm so sorry! I didn't notice you standing there. You're so quiet."

You'd think that one would kindly move out of the way after a statement like that, but no, not her. Instead, Ms. Bloom turned right back around and continued talking to Melanie. Renee just stood behind Melanie, chuckling to herself over my misery. But then, after Ms. Bloom talked Melanie's head off about restraining order this and that, she decided to walk herself and her Coco Chanel back down the hall. But, not before giving herself an improper send-off.

"Renee…Gabrielle…"

Like, what kind of greeting or goodbye, is that? Just announcing someone's name like she was the CEO of nothing important. Neither Renee nor I replied. I did one of those half-fake smiles, and Renee gave a quick thumbs up. It was nice to know that I wasn't the only one inhaling Ms. Bloom's crap.

"Well, I'm going to head to class. I'll see you guys later?" Melanie asked.

"Yes. I will see you later. And, again, I'm so sorry about yesterday," I replied.

"Stop apologizing; you have nothing to be sorry about!"

I tried to position myself for a hug, but Melanie was not going for it. I understood. I pretty much spent the entire week giving her the cold shoulder, and I guess it was time to get a taste of my own medicine. That or she was just too exhausted to pick up on my body language. Melanie just smiled and walked away, leaving Renee and me to walk together to our first-period classes. I couldn't help feeling like the worst friend, girlfriend, ever! I needed to get the advice of the one person who has known Melanie the longest. So I asked,

"Did you notice that Melanie was acting differently, or is it just me? I mean, she didn't even call me last night, but apparently, she called you. I don't know... I feel like I may have pushed her away with my issues."

"Gabrielle, Melanie's not gone; she's just been through a lot...like hell on Earth, a lot. And I know that you care for her, I can see it, and I love it! But if you're worried about losing Melanie, my advice to you is, don't. We only have like four and a half more months left in these halls. After that, most of us will never see each other again. If you think Melanie is worth it, then show her! She needs a lot more show than tell these days. Especially if you plan on getting in the ring with Ms. Bloom and earning back your title because that woman, she don't quit for nothing!"

Renee was right; Ms. Bloom was already holding the champion belt, carrying it around, and waving it in my face. Talk about show vs. tell! But sometimes, I felt like Ms. Bloom did a better job showing her love for Melanie than I did. Not to mention Ms. Bloom was THE complete package, and I was just starting to come into my own. I thought, how could I ever measure up? Especially after the way I had been treating Melanie, which wasn't even intentional. I knew I needed to redeem myself before it was too late. I needed to show Melanie just how important she was to me. Shortly after our talk, Renee and I parted ways, and I found myself bumping into the last person I expected to see, Crystal.

Crystal tried to catch an attitude as she huffed and puffed, but I put on my Gabrielle charm as I smiled and asked,

"Sorry! Have you heard anything else about the investigation?"

Crystal was at her locker, getting her books together. I was surprised that she was alone. I was so used to seeing her with Jesuse or Josh.

"No, why would I know something?" Crystal asked.

"Well, remember when you got all defensive the other day over the whole Biscuit situation? I figured you might know a little bit more than the rest of us."

"Well, I don't!" Crystal replied.

Right as Crystal was about to walk away, the Devil himself appeared right before us.

"Now, did I just hear someone say my name?"

Biscuit approached with three other guys. They each had Crystal, and I surrounded. Immediately, the tiny hairs on my arms stood up. Crystal then stood face to face with Biscuit and said,

"Your little intimidation bullshit might work on everyone else around here, but I'm not afraid of you…neither one of you! Now move out of the way!"

"Oh, darn! That just means that I need to up the terror a notch or two. But no, I'm not here for you. I need to speak to Josh. Where is he?"

"At home…" Crystal dryly replied before folding her arms with her books across her chest.

"How convenient! Well, you tell Josh that whenever he decides to crawl out from underneath his bed that, I'll be waiting for him."

Biscuit glared at Crystal and me before taking a step back and releasing us from his cloud of terror. Now, that dude, he really freaked me out! Crystal started to walk away, but I still had questions.

"Wait, if Biscuit is back, then that means they still haven't found the killer. Are you sure you don't know anything?"

"We have less than two minutes before the bell rings; I can't help you. I know just as much as you do! Be grateful that we don't have to spend the rest of the school year staring at each other in the auditorium, and let the detectives figure it out!"

I finally let Crystal walk away. She insisted on not telling me anything, and no matter how frustrating that was, I decided to drop it and focus on what I could control. When I made it to my first-period Physics class and took my seat, Melanie was all I could think about. She was right to say that something changed in me the night of the dance. It did. I could never find the right time to tell her what happened after my dad picked me up from the police station. My dad has always been the type of person not to express emotion in public. No matter how upset he would get, he'd always hold his temper until we were behind closed doors.

Furious would not come close to describe my father's temperament that night. I'd say that he was more like a fuming water heater about to explode. Yeah, that would better represent the look on his face as he drove us out of the parking lot. I remember sitting in the passenger seat, feeling terrified over what he would say. But, what I didn't expect, was for him to blame it all on me and my terrible judgment.

"What in God's name were you thinking? No! What the hell were you doing out there with those other kids?"

I didn't know what to say. What could I say? That I was experiencing true love's kiss for the first time with my girlfriend?

"I was just checking on a friend."

"In the woods? Why? And which one of them is this friend? Is it the girl who came and sat next to you at the station? No, of course, it is! That's why I don't like you hanging out with those kinds of people. I mean, it could have been you instead of that, that boy! I could have lost you while you were out there doing God knows what and to God knows who..."

Okay, now, right here is when it happened. The moment I could feel my dad mentally connecting the dots. The way he dramatically paused; I could feel his energy shifting before he had a chance to finish his sentence. He looked like a dear caught in the headlights! And I knew, I just knew it was coming. My dad was so concerned with what I was doing outside behind the school instead of taking a moment to be grateful that I was still alive, that I was okay! But he didn't even ask; instead, he pulled over to the shoulder of the road, looked at me with such hostility, and asked,

What were you doing out there with that girl behind the school?"

"Nothing…we weren't doing anything besides talking."

"Just talking?" He asked.

"Yes!"

All I needed was for my dad to believe me long enough for him to drive us off the shoulder of the road and take me home. It bothered me when he'd get angry like that, which is why I never felt comfortable telling him anything. It was always his way or the highway!

"Okay, Gabrielle! I hope you're telling me the truth because I won't allow that kind of sin to live under my roof! I've told you this once before. Don't make me have to say it a third time…"

The look of repulsion not only made me feel ashamed of being gay but also for the kiss I shared with Melanie hours before. And with an ultimatum like that, I could only give him the answer he demanded. Then after it was all said and done, I hated myself for not standing up to him. It was one of those moments you replay in your mind over and over, wishing you could go back and say something differently or do something differently. The hard truth was that I couldn't! At least not at that moment. I valued having a safe, warm bed to crawl into over being true to myself. So once more, I lived another night trapped in a lie. The following morning, I was so distraught that I couldn't even make it out of bed, so I stayed home. Melanie tried reaching out, but instead of confiding in her, that's when I began pushing her away. I was embarrassed to tell her what happened. I worried she'd see me differently or decide that she didn't want to date someone with as much homophobic baggage as me. But somehow, that ended up happening anyway, which was why I needed to make things right.

While sitting in my first-period class, I thought of nothing but how I could do so. And also, Melanie, and the way she'd get this look in her eyes that would make me feel like I was the center of her entire universe. I didn't realize how much I needed her kind of love until she stopped giving it. I spent most of first period daydreaming and drawing tiny hearts around the outer edges of my book. I knew that I needed to do something; I felt it in every part of my being. I started thinking to myself; *what if my dad could just see us together, see how harmless our relationship was*, I felt that surely then, he'd have a change of heart, right? It was just mind-boggling to see how humans are more accepting of animals than each other. I seriously started to worry that maybe the animals were more intelligent than people! Because animals don't give a pigeon's turd about color, shape, size, religion, or sexuality, they are the true definition of free! Well, that is until people get involved. When will we finally learn the true value of our species? I don't think that's a question I can answer alone.

By the time lunch period arrived, I had decided to invite Melanie over to my house for dinner. It was time! Yes, I was horrified at the thought of how my father would react, but I hoped he'd learn to lead with love instead of hate. Before entering the cafeteria, I caught up with Melanie and asked to speak to her privately. I didn't want an audience with Toni and Renee sitting at the table, so I had Melanie follow me out in the hall, right in front of the cafeteria, and I asked,

"How are you feeling?"

"You know, I can't count the number of times I've been asked that question today!" Melanie replied with a smile.

"I'm sorry."

"No… don't be. I'm just trying to process a few things."

"Like what? Me?" I asked jokingly.

"Eh, you might be one of them. I don't know. My night from hell has me thinking about a lot. You shouldn't have to force yourself to come out before you're ready, and I don't think I should have to hide who I am for us to be together."

"You're right! And, that's what I wanted to tell you. Melanie, you are my light. You inspire me to think differently, to grow. Month's back, I'm pretty sure we wouldn't even be having this conversation because back then, I was okay with living a lie. But not anymore! Melanie, you are changing me and in a good way! I don't want you to think that I'm doing this just for you. I'm doing this for myself as well."

"Doing what?"

The bell sounded, and the last rush of students faded into the distance as they headed inside the cafeteria. I then gently grabbed Melanie by the hand, smiled into her deep brown eyes, and asked,

"Will you come over for dinner tonight? I want to introduce you to my dad."

Melanie then took my other hand in hers and said,

"Gabrielle, you don't have to do this."

"Melanie, I want to be with you! That's all I want more than anything! Do you even still want that?"

While waiting for a reply, I slowly pulled my hands away, fearful that Melanie was on the verge of breaking my heart. A few teachers walked by, curious about what we were doing standing in the hall. After explaining that we were on our way to lunch, Melanie and I were alone once more. I had a thought, driven by slight insecurity, and I asked jokingly yet seriously,

"I'm not losing you to Ms. Bloom, am I?"

"No, you're not losing me. But are you sure this is what you want to do?"

"I'm a billion light-years sure that I want to be with you. You're not just a high school crush or sweetheart. You're it for me. I knew it the day you chased me down, apologizing for your superficial ways. And when we talked for what felt like hours in the auditorium after I confessed my deepest secrete to you. I also knew it the moments before, during, and after our first kiss. You have my heart, Melanie. I hope that I have yours?"

I tried everything I could; I laid all of my emotions and heart on the table. I needed Melanie to know how serious I was, how I would do anything for her. In my mind, she was worth every sacrifice. Then after seconds of waiting again for a reply, Melanie stared into my eyes, grabbed me by both hands, and said,

"You have a lot more of me than you realize."

Shortly after Melanie agreed to have dinner at my house, we walked into the cafeteria and caught up with Toni and Renee. I could see that Melanie was trying, acting as if everything was okay, but she was still holding back. Melanie would barely touch me or even smile my way. I didn't want Toni or Renee to know that Melanie and I were still having trouble, so I brushed off my concern with a smile and prayed that things would get better once I finally had her at my house, sitting at the dining room table across from my dad. Sadly, with prayer, you don't always get what you ask for when you want it. I realized that all too quickly when what was supposed to be a peaceful, colorful evening turned menacing and grey.

Hours later, after being released from school, I was back at home helping my dad set the table for dinner. We lived in the same one-story house my entire life. The kitchen was green with olive paint on the cabinets and fixtures. It was a medium-sized kitchen with a yellow stove in the center to really make things pop, yuk! I asked my dad in the past if we could do a remodel on the home so that it wouldn't feel like we were stuck living 60's, but out of respect to my mom, I agreed that we'd leave everything the same. The house had been in my mother's family for three generations, and when she died, she left part of the deed to my dad. I rarely spoke about my mother; I was just five years old she died. And all I have left of her are the photos, distorted memories, and the stories my dad would tell me. He also told me how badly she wanted a baby, a daughter. But they could never get pregnant. So they talked about adoption, and that's where I entered the picture at two months old, weighing 12 lbs. and 4 oz.

As the years passed and I grew into my teens, I began feeling like my dad had regrets about adopting me. Without his wife, my mother around, I felt more like a burden than anything else. I wasn't even a year old when my mother was diagnosed with stage four colon cancer. Then four years later, she passed at 41. So often, especially now, I wondered how she felt about me being gay. Did she still love me up there in heaven? Or is she like my dad, fearful, judgmental, whispering in my ear at night that she hopes I find a nice guy to marry? Well, I just hoped that above all, my mother was proud of the person I was becoming, regardless of who I loved. As for my dad, I let him go on believing that it was Justin who I invited to dinner instead of Melanie. It was sneaky, I know! But, I just thought that once Melanie walked through the door, he would see how wonderful of a person she is, and his bias opinions would wither away. So, after setting the table, I helped my dad prepare Angus beef hamburgers, French fries, and salad. I know it's not exactly a four-star meal, but it was one of Melanie's favorites. Melanie liked her burgers with extra ketchup, mayo, mustard, onions, tomatoes, extra pickles, and lettuce! What can I say? I knew my girl well!

So after we prepared the food and poured the drinks, my dad and I sat at the table exchanging forced smiles as we waited for the doorbell to ring. I had no idea how he would react or how Melanie would. Then not even a second later, we heard knocking! Immediately, I rushed out of my seat with my heart beating uncontrollably, opened the door, and there she was; my honey buns stood before me with a bright smile and gorgeous pink tulips in her hand.

"Sorry, I'm late. I wanted to come by earlier, but I didn't want to show up empty-handed. I had no idea the store would have so many different color options."

"You're too sweet! I love tulips. You picked a good color. Come in!"

After Melanie handed me the flowers, I welcomed her inside and guided her through the house towards the dining room.

"Wow, you guys really go all out for the holidays. And wait, don't tell me, are those cookies for Santa?"

Melanie teased, but we did have the house fully decorated from the front door, throughout the living room, and back to the dining room. The house was covered in nothing but decorations. Not to mention our 7-foot Christmas tree and the fake cookies and milk that I kept sitting on top of the coffee table near the tree. So right as we walked into the dining room, I nervously smiled and formally introduced Melanie to my dad.

"Dad, this is Melanie, Melanie, this is my dad, Mr. Davis."

And the look on his face once he saw Melanie, oh it kills me to this day! I knew it was coming. I could feel his rath stretching from across the table. I was hoping he wouldn't be a bully, not in front of company. Instead, my dad just examined Melanie like a big cat in the wild as he slowly stood up.

"What's going on? That's not Justin!" He asked.

"Yeah, I know, that's the whole point! You wouldn't have agreed to any of this if I told you the truth!"

The moment was beyond awkward, especially after Melanie whispered,

"You didn't tell your dad I was coming?"

After nervously wiping away the sweat from my forehead, I tried to lighten the mood by drawing everyone's attention to the tulips. I knew that I was forcing them into an uncomfortable situation, but honestly, I didn't know any other way to bring them together.

"Dad, I'm going to put these flowers in water. I'll be right back!"

I tried to be as quick as possible as I hurried and grabbed a vase from the cabinet and ran water into it. After putting the flowers inside, I sat them in the middle of the table and asked Melanie to sit. My dad just stared back and forth between the two of us while he sat all macho at the head of the table. Mind you, this was a table for six, but the three of us quickly filled it up with the giant elephant sitting between us. Melanie and I were sitting right across from each other next to my dad. After passing the food around and filling up our plates, Melanie was the first to break the awkward silence.

"I know that you were expecting someone else to be here, but I appreciate you settling for me." Melanie slyly replied while glaring at me.

"Thank Gabrielle. I didn't really have a say in the matter."

The hostility was definitely in the air, and so was the smoke that blew out of my dad's ears. But after listening to chomping and slurping for ten minutes, Melanie tried to defuse the situation by throwing out a compliment.

"The food is delicious! I think these just might be the juiciest hamburgers I've ever had!"

Then, my dad SLAMMED his fork down onto his plate, startling Melanie with her mouth full of meat, bread, and pickles. She looked at me, then back over at my dad right as he began to shout,

"Gabrielle! What the hell is going on? Why is she in my house?"

"I was trying to tell you! I wanted you to meet the most important in my life. And she, Melanie, was just complimenting you on how delicious the burgers were..."

"STOP! I'm not goddamn senile; I know what you're trying to do! You thought you could corner me, lie to me, by parading this abomination in front of me, thinking I would somehow change my mind, my beliefs? I didn't raise you to be a manipulative liar, and I most definitely wouldn't have agreed to raise you on my own if I knew you'd turn out to be like this!"

"Whoa! You know what, I'm going to go! The hamburgers were about a six anyway, and that's being generous!" Melanie replied.

"No, don't go! The only abomination sitting at this table is you, dad! Some beliefs you have. Do you think that hating a person simply because they love differently than you gives you the right to wear the robe and carry the gavel? Even God has more heart than that. But if this God is the reason that you've become so repulsive, then I don't think that's a God I ever want know!"

The room stood quiet. It was the longest minute of my life. I was surprised when Melanie opened her mouth and said,

"I really care for Gabrielle, deeply. I'd do anything to protect her, keep her happy. Yes, I am gay, but I'm not a monster!"

"Are you calling me a monster? In my own house!" My dad shouted.

"No...you missed my..."

"Gabrielle, please escort your friend from the table and out of my house. Oh, and by the way, I heard that your mom is finally out of prison. That's wonderful news. Tell her that I understand everything now, and I'll be praying that she gets it right this second time around. Now, that's me being generous!"

"Wow! Well after a comment like that...I hope she does too! Because this world, it doesn't deserve my kind of love. And I can see myself out!" Melanie replied.

The way that Melanie stared at my dad, I felt her heart-ripping breaking mine in the process. My dad just shrugged it off and continued eating while Melanie took one last look at me before storming out of the dining room. I went to follow, but my dad had more to say.

"You can go upstairs and pack your bags. You're no longer welcome here!"

"Do you really think that is going to work? It might have worked last week, but now, I'm seven days wiser. This house belongs to me just as much as it does to you, if not more. After you threatened to put me out on the streets a second time, I had a meeting with the family lawyer. My mother left me a large share of this house. So if I were you, I wouldn't continue to cross me. Otherwise, it will be you who ends up underneath a bridge with a suitcase full of clothes."

I was disgusted, completely, and utterly disgusted. I tried to catch up to Melanie after leaving my dad sitting alone with a mouth full of fries. I found Melanie standing on the corner, just two houses away from mine. I felt terrible because it was freezing outside, and she was just standing there shivering.

"Melanie, I'm so, so sorry. Please forgive me! I didn't think he'd react like that or say the things he said..."

"It's not your fault. You tried! And you didn't even have to do that."

Melanie was devastated, I could tell. Even though she tried to put on a brave face, I could see beyond it. Melanie then began pacing the corner as if she was trying to figure out which way to go. I followed trying to calm her down. Once I got Melanie to stop and look at me for a second, I gently grabbed both her hands to warm her up. Melanie, however, couldn't stand still long enough for me to comfort her as she continued panicking and looking around frantically.

"I'm okay, Gabrielle. I just need to figure out what I'm going to do. I don't want to call Ms. Bailey to pick me up and have to explain this… I think I'm just going to walk. Yeah… I'm going to walk home!"

As Melanie glanced my way again, staring intensely into my eyes, I felt a drop of snow land on my cheek.

"Melanie, it's cold out here, and now it's starting to snow! I can walk you to the bus stop and wait with you. I think there's a bus stop down the street. I don't want you to walk home and get sick out here."

"It's okay. I want to walk. This coat is warmer than it looks."

If I had to walk with Melanie to the nearest bus stop and wait until I knew she was safe, then that's what I was going to do. Even if all I had was my blue jean pants and a cardigan to keep me warm, I knew my dad would be upset, but boy, was I completely was thrown off by his ignorance and lack of respect. The principles he supposedly held near, and dear to his heart went right out of the window when he saw Melanie. I only wondered what she was thinking, how she was feeling.

I knew it wasn't good. But I hoped that she wouldn't let my bigot of a father come between us through it all.

SUCH A PREDICAMENT I've gotten myself into! Gabrielle kept begging me to let her walk with me to the bus stop. I finally just pulled her in close and gave her the tightest hug, goodbye that I could. Then, I insisted that I needed to walk home alone, to clear my mind. I could see how much she cared and how heartbroken she was over it all. Her dad and my mom must have been spun straight out of a special place in hell. For a person to allow that much hate to live inside them and not even realize it or give a damn, I found that to be the most heartbreaking. So after leaving Gabrielle standing on the corner with a kiss on the forehead, I turned around and began my journey back home.

After walking a couple of blocks down the street, I got winded from all the festering emotions inside me. I felt alone, and the empty streets weren't making it any better. It felt as if the last bit of light left inside me was being sucked out. Between my mother, Ms. Bailey and Jesuse, and then Gabrielle and her demon father, I was mentally drained. When I finally arrived at a bus stop across from Dave's Cleaners, I took a seat on the cold hard bench and got lost in the cloud of snow hovering above me. I decided I would take the bus home after all. Still, as quickly as I had that thought, I remembered that Jesuse was making himself nice and cozy in the place that used to be my joy. So, I imagined a new idea while staring up at the white sky. There was only one person I could think of besides Renee, who showed me true devotion, care, and concern. It was the only person who, ironically, I trusted to make me feel better. The only person I desired to make me feel better. I decided to give this person a call and was surprised by how quickly she answered but grateful overall.

I waited fifteen minutes in the cold before my ride showed up. When she finally did, I lit up when I heard the tires pulling up to the curb. I quickly jumped in the car and warmed my hands in front of the vents. I then looked over to my left, trying hard not to break down, and I said while shivering,

"Thank you for coming all this way to get me."

"No problem! It didn't even take me ten minutes. How long were you sitting out there anyway? And what were you doing over here on this side of town?"

I hesitated to reply for apparent reasons. But I was too mentally exhausted to think up a lie.

"I was with Gabrielle. She invited me over for dinner, which lasted not even five minutes before her dad... things just didn't go as planned. I'm sorry, I know that's not what you want to hear right now."

"No, I appreciate the honesty. And I'm sorry things didn't work out. But, life is all about making mistakes and learning from them. Eventually, you'll learn who's good for you and who's... not."

I was baffled by how calm Ms. Bloom was. I was expecting her to at least be offended. Maybe she was. Perhaps that was her new way of telling me off in disguise.

"Can we go to your house?" I asked.

"It's a school night, Melanie, and you don't even have a change of clothes. I think it would be better if I dropped you off at home, considering."

"Please, I'm not ready to go back home yet. I was supposed to be out for another hour or two anyway. And with Jesuse..."

"Ah, I see... I imagine that must be hard for you to accept."

"What do you mean?"

"Ms. Bailey and I are much closer than you think. But, listen, it's almost 7 o'clock. Did you get full over at Gabrielle's? You look like you're hungry."

"I lost my appetite, but I think I can find it again if you're cooking?"

"Well, I haven't had dinner yet either. So, this is what we'll do; I will drive us to my house, whip up something scrumptious. While I'm cooking, you can fill me in on everything that's been going on with you, including whatever happened here tonight. Then after we eat, I'll take you home. Sound like a plan?"

A terrific plan it was, and I agreed. Ms. Bloom and I continued our small talk for another 7 minutes until we got to her house. Once inside, we immediately went to the kitchen, washed our hands, and snacked on cheese and grapes while deciding what to fix for dinner. After taking fifteen minutes to decide between tacos and spaghetti, we chose homemade pizza. Funny, it wasn't even an option, but I could tell that just like me, Ms. Bloom was quite indecisive. I also admired how she kept her kitchen stocked with fresh veggies, canned goods, and lots of fruits.

I then began thinking to myself how, not even an hour before Ms. Bloom picked me up, I was being treated worse than an animal. The words Gabrielle's dad uttered burned into my brain like a disease. But being with Ms. Bloom, I suddenly felt alive again, like I was a human worthy of being treated with respect and dignity. I know that we've had our ups and downs, but Ms. Bloom never wavered in her love for me. She was in my corner no matter what. And the way Ms. Bloom smiled as we both tossed our pizza dough warmed my insides. I couldn't understand how she still had the heart to care for me after I betrayed her more than once. I began feeling many emotions at once. While Ms. Bloom was smiling from ear to ear, I was breaking down from the inside out. That long-awaited weeping finally emerged as I took a step back against the island countertop and let myself fall to the ground. Ms. Bloom immediately stopped what she was doing to kneel in front of me, and wipe my tears.

"I'm sorry... I was trying really hard not to cry, but... it's just, I've been through so much, I can't take it anymore."

"Hey, it's okay. I'm here. It's okay to cry." She replied while pulling me close for a hug.

"I don't understand. I mean, through it all, you're the only person that's stuck by me. Why? After everything I put you through?"

"Because, believe it or not, Melanie, I do love you! You remind me a lot of myself when I was your age. You're special, not only to me but to your friends and Ms. Bailey as well. So don't waste this time being angry with her for taking Jesuse in."

"It's not just that she took him in. It's that she didn't even think to talk to me about it first. And while I was missing, instead of searching for me, she was just replacing me."

"Melanie, I know you don't believe that. Ms. Bailey loves you so much, more than you realize. She was panicked the rest of the day, calling your cell, calling the police every hour, if not half an hour. Ms. Bailey could never replace you. Her heart's way too big for that," Ms. Bloom replied, then slowly sat next to me.

"I don't know… You're the only person who makes me feel irreplaceable."

"Because you are! And not just to me! So, what happened with you and Gabrielle?"

"It was her dad; I don't want to talk about it. After he threatened me…"

"Wait, he threatened you? What did he say?"

Ms. Bloom grew furious as she repositioned herself in front of me, waiting for me to say,

"Nothing! I don't want to talk about Gabrielle or her dad. I'm starting to think that maybe you've been right this whole time about everything."

"No, I want you to tell me what this man said! Because if I need to loosen a few of his tightly wound screws, I will!"

"Please, I've felt enough pain this week to last the next two years. The only thing I want right now is to feel good, loved! I need to feel something real. I need to feel you…"

I tried reaching in for a kiss as Ms. Bloom was just inches away from me. I could smell her ginger mint breath on my nose. I could also tell she was holding back as she softly whispered,

"No. I can't. Not like this. I don't want you to think of me as…"

"Please…" I begged.

I gently pulled her closer as I placed my hand on the back of her head, feeling her soft hair. Our lips were then centimeters apart. I felt the trembling rolling through her body, her breath, as she tried to resist my gravitational pull. But just like everything else on Earth, it eventually lands where it's supposed to, and she landed right onto me. I loved feeling her lips intertwining with mine. The perfect amount of saliva that she'd leave on my bottom lip after firmly holding for seconds at a time pulled me in even more. It was the most intense, deep, most yearned for kiss I had in a while. Then as she leaned closer, pressing her body against mine, squeezing my arms from the pleasure she felt, she suddenly let go, and said,

"I've missed you so much... But we can't. I can't. You're hurting. And I told you that you need to make a choice!"

"I'm making it! Don't fight it, just let me show you!"

I slowly got up from the kitchen floor and stood just above her, reaching out my hand. The way she looked at me with hesitation and want, I knew she couldn't deny herself much longer. So, I smiled, and she smiled back, grabbing my hand while slowly standing up, right in front of me. We then walked upstairs to the bedroom and completely forgot about the oven warming itself to 450 degrees and the pizzas. When I said I found my appetite, I didn't know that deep down; I meant my hunger for her. Then as I was standing at the foot of her king-sized bed, I could feel the moisture between us both building, and she said,

"I do care about you, Melanie. I care about your feelings, your mind, and your heart. Are you sure that this is what you want? There's no rewriting this part of our story once we cross this line. And I don't share this part of myself with just anyone. Sex is very intimate, special, and it should be for you as well."

I trusted Ms. Bloom, and the fact that she treasured her body, herself, gave me the extra validation that I needed. Yes, we've been physical in the past. But the two-handed foreplay was nothing compared to what we were about to explore with one another. I was opening a new door to Pandora's box, and though I was nervous as hell, it made it that much more exiting. The light from the hallway lit a corner of the room, just enough for us to see each other, our expressions, enough for me to see how badly she wanted me. After removing my top and then removing hers, we slowly undressed each other with our eyes and our hands.

My heart began to race as we stood there exposed. I gazed upon her perfect and delicious breasts and froze. She then stepped closer, grabbed my left hand, and placed it over her right breast. And as she worked my palm over the tip of her nipple, I slowly regained my confidence. Moments later, we were underneath the covers, inhaling and exhaling the heat that surrounded us. I was filled with more power as she caressed her body gently over mine while melting herself in and around my body. Then as I got lost into her eyes, eyes that spoke to me a new language, I was pleasantly surprised as we zealously ascended into a whole new dimension together. Another hour later, we had ascended twice more.

I didn't have any words. I was speechless as we laid together with our bodies intertwined. I had never been with anyone sexually before. I had no idea how good it would feel to be, loved. At least that's what I thought it was in the moment. And for the first time in a long time, I wasn't afraid or worried. I was simply relieved and, in more ways, than one.

"How do you feel?" She asked.

"I feel like I'm in a dream."

"Well, you're not dreaming. If you are, then that means I am too, and this was the best REM sleep I've had in years."

"Really?" I asked with a smile.

Ms. Bloom reached in for a kiss, and for a moment, I thought we were going for round four. But instead, she slowly pulled back and said with a smirk,

"You're stuck with me now, darling. And I hope you're still hungry because I'm starving!"

After holding each other a few moments more, we went downstairs to finish making our pizzas. It's crazy the effect this woman had on me because I not once thought about Gabrielle. Not until after the fact, after it was too late. And I think the worst part of it all was knowing that if I had thought about Gabrielle, it wouldn't have changed a thing. So what did that say about me? Who was I becoming? I'm not a cheater. I can't stand cheaters. But I think in my mind, part of me believed Gabrielle and I's relationship couldn't survive her dad and the evils in the world. And if I were going to be with Ms. Bloom, then she would be end game. And with that thought, I knew I'd have to prepare for the most heartbreaking conversation of my life.

As the night for Ms. Bloom and I came to an end, I worried about what Friday would bring. I felt like I had created a mess, a mess that I wasn't quite ready to clean up. After enjoying freshly baked miniature pizzas with ham, extra pineapples, mushrooms, and peppers on mine, Ms. Bloom dropped me off at the corner down the street from Ms. Bailey's house. It was a quarter to ten when I arrived, and before getting out of the car, I embraced her touch one last time and savored the succulence of her lips. We said our goodbyes, and I walked five houses down the street until I reached home. Ms. Bailey would usually leave the door unlocked when she knew that I'd be out late. So I was surprised when I went to twist the nob that the door didn't budge! But more surprised when I saw who opened the door after knocking and ringing the doorbell for what felt like ten minutes.

"Why did you lock the door?" I shouted.

"I always lock the door at night. You were supposed to be back here two hours ago," Jesuse replied.

I brushed my way inside, past Jesuse, turned around, and said,

"I know that you've only been crashing here for a couple of days now, but we don't lock the doors until everyone is home. If you're going to bombard me with your presence, at least have the decency to humble yourself!"

"Look, I'm not trying to cause any trouble. I'm just looking out for Ms. Bailey. With what I just went through, I don't feel comfortable being in a house and not protecting it."

"Well, next time your feeling scary, lock your bedroom door. But, leave the front door unlocked, please!"

I started to walk away towards my room, and then Jesuse stopped me by saying,

"I covered for you…just so you know."

"What?" I asked in confusion.

"Um, Gabrielle? She called here a while ago asking if you made it home safe. She said she tried calling you but didn't get an answer. So I told her and Ms. B that you were over Renee's house cooling off. You're welcome!"

"I don't need your help, and I sure as hell didn't ask for it!"

"Oh really? I mean because that Coco Chanel is, whew, pretty damn strong. I think my mother used to buy that from time to time now that I think of it."

Jesuse stood there smiling as if he was waiting for the, *Most Clever Person of The Year* award. It was late, and I was growing furious by the second. I just look at him and said,

"Why don't you focus on picking out the right tombstone for your mother and worry about yourself? Can you do that?"

"Wow! Well, thanks for caring, but my mother's body is being cremated. I pick up her ashes tomorrow."

"That's wonderful! Now you can keep her with you forever!"

I started to walk away again, but Jesuse stopped me one last time by saying,

"You'll never understand true loss until you've known true love."

I didn't get it at the time, but his comment did give me a slight pause. Before he could share another one of his messages sent down from Buddha or whoever, I hurried up the stairs before he could whisper another word. And I know how it looks; you probably think I was a complete ass, right? I understood he was grieving the death of his mother, but the fact of the matter was, Jesuse was a bully! He was nasty to me my entire high school experience, spreading his homophobic gospel. And was I supposed to just forget about all of that, let it all go because his mother died? I couldn't ignore the truth. I couldn't let down my guard because I knew deep down in his heart that he didn't give a damn about me. So why should I give a damn about him? I sure as hell wasn't going to be like

Ms. Bailey and tend to his every need, no! Jesuse got an, oh no, sad face from me on Monday, and Tuesday, it was back to black.

After showering and getting ready for bed, I checked my phone and saw that I had ten missed calls and seven voicemails from Gabrielle. I felt terrible. I knew that she was worried out of her mind, but I couldn't call her back. I needed time to figure out how I would explain my actions. I loved Gabrielle; at least, I thought that I did. If love causes you to do stupid things like what I did, maybe my love for her was valid. But, on the other hand, perhaps I was just a complete mess and couldn't handle my life spinning out of control. Or maybe I was just a girl in love with two amazing people. I think it was possibly all of the above that troubled me. Either way, I knew that Gabrielle deserved to know the truth, but what parts of that truth I would disclose, and which parts I would keep buried in my memory, well, that was the question that kept me awake throughout the night.

| 7 |

THE PRICE

IT WAS barely 6:30 A.M., and the sun was still hiding behind the moon when I heard heavy footsteps above me, pacing back and forth. Melanie had woken me up from another dream I was having about my mother. *Thank God it's Friday.* I said to myself as I took a deep breath and removed the covers away from my body. It was also the last day of school before Christmas break, and I looked forward to being able to sleep in, undisturbed for the next three weeks. But, of course, I couldn't complain too much. Ms. Bailey was the only reason I had a warm room, bed, and a place to call home. Even though it did take lots of convincing for Ms. Bailey to get me to agree to leave the only home I'd known most of my life, I knew deep down she was right.

It was Wednesday afternoon when Ms. Bailey showed up on my doorstep with Crystal awkwardly standing by her side. I was on my way out, which was probably the only reason I even answered the door. Ms. Bailey looked so concerned. She didn't even need to open her mouth. I knew just what she was doing. I tried to make it short, explain to both of them that I was running late for an appointment, but Crystal could smell my bullshit a mile away. After they spent ten minutes trying to convince me to stay and talk, I walked Crystal and Ms. B into the living room, where they both sat on the sofa. I then flopped down on my mom's recliner and waited for Ms. Bailey to say,

"Jesuse, I know that you're in a hurry. I won't stay for long. But I heard from some of your classmates that you've been struggling. So first, I want you to know how sorry I am for your loss. You've been in my prayers every night since. And I want you to know that you're not alone, Jesuse. What are your plans, as far as your living situation goes and school?"

"Why? Did Crystal tell you that I'm living here without power and food?"

"Jesuse, I was just worried about you! I'm sorry, but I couldn't let you live like this until Monday," Crystal interrupted.

"I thought I already told you that I didn't need your help!" I sternly replied.

Ms. Bailey then glanced at the two of us before saying,

"Okay, Jesuse... that's fine. Just, please don't be upset with Crystal. I only came over here out of genuine concern for you. I tell you kids all the time that you're more than just students to me; you're family. And when family is hurting, you show up. I, too, lost someone when I was young, my grandpa. He died fighting for equal rights in a five-day-long protest in Alabama. He protested for us to live in a world free from hatred and discrimination, only for us to end up still living in that world fighting for rights fought fifty years ago. Then when my grandfather got shot in the chest, not a single person stopped to help. Instead, they continued marching and protesting, walking around us like we weren't even there. I had to watch him die on the ground with my tiny hands pressed against his heart. I was just a child, not much younger than you."

Ms. Bailey continued trying to reason with me, bridging the gap of understanding. Then out of nowhere, I broke out into tears. Hearing her speak about her grandpa and then re-seeing my mom's face covered in blood, I couldn't handle it. I lost it!

"I'm just so tired of crying... I'm tired of feeling this much pain."

It was humiliating having Crystal and Ms. Bailey stare at me with such sadness in their eyes. I tried to contain myself, but it only made me weep more.

"Jesuse...can I hug you? Can I just..."

Ms. Bailey couldn't even complete her sentence. Instead, she just walked toward me with open arms, and I let her embrace me. I got the sense that a warm, hold me until the tears on my cheeks dried was exactly the kind of hug I needed.

"It's gonna be okay," she whispered.

After what felt like a good five minutes of relief, Ms. Bailey looked at me and said,

"You are going to be okay! You have everything inside of you to make it through this. You have courage; you have strength; you have love! You are going to be okay. Would you like to come over for dinner? I'm making wings, macaroni and cheese, and green beans?"

Well, I wasn't going to turn down a warm meal, especially after eating cold cans of soup for the past couple of days. Ms.

Bailey said that she would see what she could do to help me out. With me turning eighteen in a few months and not having any other family around, I liked the idea of becoming emancipated. But I knew it would be a long shot seeing as I didn't have a job. Then later that night, Ms. Bailey said that she would ask the judge to grant her temporary guardianship until I turned eighteen. I prayed like hell that I wouldn't end up in some foster home with a total stranger. I even swore I'd abide by her rules and promised to do extra chores around the house since I wasn't working or going to school at the time.

I remember Ms. Bailey spent the rest of the evening checking on me and checking her phone because Melanie was missing. I admired Ms. Bailey for her humbleness and generosity. She opened up a new part of my heart. Just seeing how someone, a stranger, could be so kind, for me, was difficult to believe. It just seems like nowadays, if someone does something nice for you, they almost always want something in return. But not Ms. B; she was a whole new kind of breed. I could tell how sincere of a person she was after that hug. And honestly, it was probably the most heartfelt hug I've ever had in my life, besides from my mom, of course.

I wondered to myself; *what would the world be like, if everyone had a piece of Ms. Bailey inside them?* I didn't want to wonder for too long, I decided that I would try learning from the best, and maybe, just maybe, I would start to heal if I hadn't begun too already. Now, back to Friday, I was in bed, waiting for Melanie to go to the restroom before I could get up and speak to Ms. Bailey. See, here's the thing, and yes, it gets a little tricky because although I wanted to become humbler and kinder, like Ms. Bailey. I still had that rational, vengeful, tormented part of me that was determined to make Fernando pay. I needed to avenge my mother's death, to bring her justice. All I had to do was get Fernando alone. But the only problem with that was, the son of a bitch was never alone.

So I needed to watch Fernando, follow him, sunrise to sunset, and catch that fucker in a vulnerable place at a vulnerable time. Unfortunately, the city bus, and my mountain bike, wasn't apt for the job. I needed a car. And that's where my beloved Ms. B came in. After quickly putting on my clothes, fixing my hair, and removing the sleep around my eyes, I went into the kitchen where Ms. Bailey was packing her lunch, and I said,

"Good morning, uh, do you need any help?"

"Oh, good morning Jesuse, no, I'm fine. Thanks for asking. Did you sleep okay?"

"Yes, I did...thank you! I just wanted to ask you something, and I completely understand if you say no, you've done so much for me already. And I don't want to."

"What is it, Jesuse?" Ms. Bailey asked with a smile.

"Can I borrow your car today? I have my license, and..."

"My car? What do you need my car for?"

"Well, I pick up my mother's ashes today. I was hoping I could go somewhere, to the river, and have a small ceremony, by myself. It's hard sometimes trying to get around, waiting for the buses. I'll have your car back to you before school gets out. But, I understand if it's too much to ask."

I watched as Ms. Bailey hesitated, then walked to the refrigerator to grab an apple. She then turned toward me and asked,

"What time are you going to pick up your mother's ashes?"

"I was going to leave around 9:00 or 9:30!"

It was the truth! I did plan to pick up my mom's ashes, but the time, well, that depended on Fernando and whether or not I could catch him alone. If by noon I had nothing, I planned on picking up my mother's ashes and getting back to school in time just before the final bell. As I waited for a reply, my heart rate kicked up because I knew that Melanie would fly out of the bathroom at any moment. For the past couple of mornings, she'd spend about five to ten minutes at a time in there, doing whatever it is that girls do. I couldn't focus; my clock was running out, and as I waited to read Ms. Bailey's lips for a yes or no answer, she surprised me when she said,

"Okay! You can come pick up the car after first period. I'll let Principal Settle know that you're coming. Do you know where the teacher's lounge is?"

"Yes...I think so..."

"It's the door to the left of the cafeteria. I'll be in there."

"Thanks so much, Ms. B! I promise I'll bring your car back before school's out!"

"You better have my car parked in the parking lot before 2:45 P.M.! I know I only live about five minutes away, but I'm not walking anywhere in this cold weather! And, I inspect my car every morning, so I'll know if anything is out of place."

"I promise, I'll take good care of it! And I would never have you walking alone on the cold hard sidewalk. Thank you so much! I'll be there at 8:50 A.M.!"

I tried to hurry back to my room before Melanie and I made eye contact. Thankfully, she opened the bathroom door right as I was closing mine. Part of me felt horrible for intruding in her space. I didn't want to have another silent argument; I needed to have a clear mind for what I was about to do. I stayed in the room until Melanie and Ms. Bailey left for school, and I fixed myself a bowl of cereal and toast. I wanted just enough food in my stomach to get me energized for the day.

By the time 8:40 A.M. arrived, I was ready and on my way. When I got to school, I was surprised by how much things have changed. When I came before, I wasn't as alert. But this day, I could see how James's murder really affected things. It almost looked like a prison with the number of guards posted at each door. The school even had a couple of squad cars parked out front. And one of the officers recognized me as I made my way to the top of the stairs.

"Jesuse? I'm surprised to see you back here so soon."

"Yeah, well, I couldn't hide in the house forever."

I didn't plan on telling him shit. The last thing I needed was for the cops to be on my case, stalking me around town. If I was going to catch Fernando alone, I needed to be almost invisible.

When I made my way towards the entrance of the school, security was hungry to search me. I guess it was a good thing I was already prepared and left my gun at home. No, not Ms. B's house, but my house. And speaking of houses, I had no idea what was going to come of our house. It was solely in my mother's name and long paid off. I thought that with me being her only family, her only kid, the house would go to me. But I had a feeling that some real-estate agent would be snooping around trying to make a sale. Or do whatever real estate agents do when a person suddenly dies and the house becomes vacant. I couldn't even afford to pay the taxes.

The idea of getting a job was starting to sound better and better by the day. Once I was inside the building and cleared, I made my way to the teacher's lounge and waited outside the door until the bell rang. Thinking I would be in and out with no problems, I ran into the one person who was the cause of most of mine, Josh. He was surprisingly walking alone, and the way he looked at me was like he'd just seen a ghost. I didn't get it; Josh's whole demeanor was different. I tried to look away, pretending like I didn't notice him. Then right when I looked back, Josh approached and asked,

"Hey, what are you doing here? I thought you were on like, bereavement leave or something."

"I am…so, don't worry! I won't be here for long."

"Who says I'm worried? I'm not worried about anything."

"Are you sure? Because it's your face that's saying otherwise."

"Jesuse!" Ms. Bailey shouted.

Finally! My body temperature was starting to drop just from looking at Josh. I didn't know what his deal was or who or what had him scared shitless, but I had my own demons to slay, which is why I was so grateful when Ms. Bailey handed me her deep green teddy bear-shaped key chain. I felt like I was about to go on a treasure hunt. All I needed was some trail mix and Gatorade. I regained a purpose for living as I casually tried to make my way back down the hall. Curiosity's a bitch, though, and it got me taking one last glance at Josh before turning the corner. I wanted to say something, but this inner voice inside told me to keep on moving. So I walked away, leaving Josh to sort out the skeletons in his locker.

I DIDN'T know what to say. I mean, what could I say? My guilt was starting to catch up to me. But, I couldn't stop myself from ogling. The past couple of days had me thinking a lot about the actions that led me to be scared shitless everywhere I turned. Then, heading to second period and running into Biscuit and his crew reaffirmed that feeling for me.

"Joshy, my buddy! I'm so glad that you finally decided to crawl out from underneath your bed and face me like an adult. So tell me, how's living life in torment and guilt treating you?"

Biscuit surrounded me by four of his loyal members, and suddenly, I felt like trout in water. Biscuit knew how to intimidate someone without making it evident to the people looking around. He'd smile a giant ass fake smile, position his arms to his side like he wasn't a threat when in reality, that's all that he was. I didn't want to give him the satisfaction of proving him right, letting him see right through to my insecurities. So I put on the same fake smile and pretended like I was oblivious.

"Hey, man, I'm just enjoying my freedom! It's a beautiful day to be alive; no regrets on my end!"

I tried to brush past Biscuit and his sausages, but not surprisingly, they tightened the gap.

"Oh no, no, no Josh! You're not going to get away that easily. I have plans for you, and I intend to carry out those plans very soon. I'm not sure what to be most angry about, though; the fact that you tried to infiltrate my group by speaking badly about me or that you tried to have me thrown in jail. Tsk-tsk, you crumbled the wrong Biscuit buddy. But don't fret. I promise to make sure that you atone for your sins."

Biscuit then stepped aside, allowing me to pass. Then after taking just five steps ahead, Biscuit shouted,

"You should have stayed underneath the bed where the monsters can't get to you!"

I just kept walking while the snickering faded to silence. I tried to wipe it out of my mind, tell myself that it was all just a bunch of hogwash. And when I finally got to second period and had a chance to sit down and open up my book, I became furious. Just thinking about where I was status-wise, not even two weeks before then. I went from being the predator to being the prey. How dramatically the roles reversed! And I didn't understand how it happened. Though there is a large piece of information that I did leave out. Besides trying to get Biscuit to take the fall for James's murder, I was also trying to get him voted out of his own group.

The afternoon when Biscuit was taken into custody, Wednesday evening to be exact, I went to the meeting spot where his loyal twenty had gathered. They were all at Franklin's place, one of Biscuit's closest members. I got the information from Franklin during seventh period that day. He encouraged me to stop by and say my peace. I figured I could talk some sense into the guys. I thought that if I could reason with them, get them to understand that violence wasn't the solution, then maybe they'd agree to find a less gruesome way to be heard. Franklin was eager to get me to stand up and speak. For a moment, it felt like he was really on my side, the only person on my side. And before I knew it, all eyes were on me, and the words were coming out of my mouth faster than I could stop them.

"Hey, guys! I don't know what to say other than I was raised catholic. And I know I don't exactly look like the religious type, but I do believe in God. I believe in sin. I mean, Biscuit wanted me to murder a fifty-year-old woman, a mother, who was already dying. Like seriously? What are we? That's not how you fight for justice! That's not how you make your voice heard! Biscuit, he's reckless, he's sloppy, and he's a goddamn monster! A monster who will one day be taken down, if not by the system, then by someone off the streets. And if you continue to follow him, he will lead you off of a fucking cliff! Is that what you want? No! We need to think smart, be smart! We make real change by getting into these positions of power and attacking the system from within. Now, who's with me?"

I waited and waited, and waited, for what felt like an eternity. It was so quiet that I felt like I could hear the crickets chirping in the backyard. Then suddenly, one of the guys in the group stood up and approached me. I was nervous because not a single person appeared enthused by what I said. Even Franklin surprised me as he sat there with his head held down in shame. Then while the guy was standing next to me, a no-name I'd never paid attention to before, he pulled me in close and said,

"I think you should leave...now. And if I were you, I wouldn't mention this night to anyone. Most of us here knew Biscuit long before he became, Biscuit. You only know the stories, but we were there. We were willing to hear you, but we can't support anyone who disrespects our brother. So go home, Josh, and watch your back."

I was shocked, absolutely shocked! I figured it would be challenging to try and convince a few of them, but all of them? I was stunned. I took one last glance over at Franklin, and I walked out, leaving my pride behind. I didn't intend to throw Biscuit's name under the bus as I did. I was just trying to prove my point, get them on my side, and see that I was one of them, but smarter! After that, I felt like I had lost everything. First, I lost my position on the football team to Derek fucking Washington. My girlfriend of six years to, Jesuse. My parents were divorcing during the worst possible time in my life. And lastly, I lost my power, my pride, and my second home. I was done, exhausted, and out of solutions.

I know I've done a tone of bad shit in my life, but being a killer, now that's one thing I could proudly say I wasn't. But at the same time, a small part of me believed that maybe I was at least capable. I mean, I showed up to do the job. Perhaps I had the serial killer gene after all. And even just believing that I could hold that kind of power inside me, the hatred that would allow me to overlook my values, well, that scared the shit out of me. So I just sat there in my second-period class, reminiscing on everything that's happened in the year, not hearing a word my teacher said. And sadly, when class came to an end, the rest of the day sped up as well. Typically, yes, I'd be excited, hell any teenager would be. But the conversation that I had with Biscuit earlier left a sour taste in my mouth that traveled its way to my chest, giving me heartburn. I had a strong feeling that Biscuit was out looking for revenge and that I was overdue for a taste of my own medicine.

I was on my way to my car when Biscuit and his different group of guys appeared, marching their way towards me. I guess he liked to rotate out his gang like he did his guns. But right when I went to open my car door, one of the guys quickly ran up and immediately slammed the door back shut. As they surrounded me, I calmly turned to them and said,

"Listen, I don't want any trouble. It's Christmas break. Can we just... have a heart?"

Biscuit then stood closer, making his way front and center, and said,

"I told you, Josh, I have plans for you, special plans that I intend to carry out today!"

Biscuit smiled as he stood inches away from me, then turned to one of the guys and said,

"Hey, isn't there like some park nearby?"

"Yeah, you mean the one with the broken swings? It's like a couple of blocks away."

"Oh, perfect! Come on, Joshy, let's take a walk."

"No, that's okay. I'm fine right here. Whatever you need to say or do, you can do it right here."

"I see that you nursed one of your balls back to health during class. How sweet! But uh, I wasn't asking."

Before I knew it, another one of the other guys kneed me in my groin and snatched my car keys right out of my hand. It was clear from then on that I really didn't have a choice but to do what they said. Now here's where I'll need to become a bit more descriptive, just to make it easier for you to keep up with what happened next. So there's Biscuit, who you already know. Then there was Droopy and Hairy. Hairy was the guy who warned me to go home Wednesday night;

he pretty much gave me the boot from the group after I was silently voted out. Droopy was this other douche with red, crusty tired-looking eyes, but he had more veins in his arms than a body builder. And lastly, there was Popeye and Slender Kid. Now, these two dopes looked just as their nicknames describe. Popeye dressed like a 60's sailor, and Slender kid was the height of a tree and the size of the light pole in front of me.

Alright, I was probably dramatic with how I described Slender Kid, but he was extremely tall and dangerously skinny. Now here's when the fun part began. While awkwardly walking through the school parking and grass to the sidewalk, we crossed the street and continued to the park. That's when, for the first time, I became fearful for my life. It was roughly 40 degrees outside, but the chill didn't stop me from building up a sweat. Biscuit led the group while the other guys walked beside me, two on each side with one following behind the other. I tried to get Biscuit's attention to talk some sense into him, but I was quickly running out of time.

"Hey, come on, Biscuit, I didn't mean anything by what I said. I was just pissed! You don't have to do this. Come on!"

Biscuit continued walking to the park without saying a word. Once we were there, I watched as he looked around, checking if any neighbors or kids were around. Oddly, the park was empty. I guess not a lot of people enjoyed being outside during the winter. And the part of the park where we were was out of view from most of the houses. There was a jungle gym in front of us and the broken swings to the right of it. Biscuit stood near the center of the jungle gym while the other guys stood close to me. I stared right into Biscuit's eyes, waiting for him to say something. But, with one quick nod of the head, Biscuit gave out his orders, and Slender Kid grabbed both of my arms, holding them behind my back as he forced me to the ground. Then Popeye grabbed my legs, and they both laid me on the grass with my stomach exposed.

I tried to kick and squirm free, but before I could even inhale the cold air once more, Droopy kicked me on my side with his rugged leather boot, and then Hairy struck me on my other. After playing soccer with my ribs, Slender Kid grabbed me by the arms and sat me up in a sitting position. When I thought the torturing nightmare was ending, Hairy came up and decked me across the face causing the blood inside my veins to fly right out of my nose. Then again, with another strike to the jaw and another across my cheekbone. While my face was becoming an abstract painting, my ribs were barely hanging on. I was sure I was going to die; I knew it! While barely seeing through my right eye, I glanced up at Biscuit, who was standing there with his arms crossed, smiling. I tried begging for them to stop, but the torture only continued, that was until Biscuit gave another signal.

Then finally, it stopped! I let myself fall back to the ground. I was so exhausted from the beatings that I couldn't even move. Next thing I knew, Biscuit was walking towards me, kneeling with a wretched smile, saying,

"I wish it didn't have to end this way, Josh. But you betrayed my trust. You tried to make a fool out of me. You did! I couldn't just let you get away with that untouched. But you were right about one thing; I am a monster. Life made me this way! And you made me do this! Look, I can see that you're a little beat up right now. If you want, I can give you a five-minute break to catch your breath?"

I could barely move, let alone speak. Then Biscuit turned to the guys and said,

"Nah, I'd rather finish this now! Grab his arms and legs and make sure he doesn't move!"

"Wait...pul-plea-please..." I pleaded.

After Slender Kid and Droopy followed his orders, Biscuit took his right foot and placed it over my neck. And as he pressed down, I struggled to say,

"I can... can't...Brea..."

"You can't what? Breathe? Oh shucks, now you sound just like another one of those..."

Before Biscuit could finish his sentence, I heard a familiar voice shout out,

"STOP! LET HIM GO!"

I couldn't see because I could barely move my head. But as the voice continued speaking, I figured out exactly who it was. I didn't know whether to be embarrassed, upset, or thankful. I was in too much pain to think about it.

"Wow! Look, Joshy! It's your boyfriend coming to save the day. Damn! If only he knew."

"Let him go!" Jesuse demanded.

"Or you'll do what?" Biscuit replied.

All I could feel was Biscuit's shoe pressing deeper into my neck. Then out of nowhere, I heard the sound of gunfire shooting into the air, and I listened as the footsteps came closer and prayed that Biscuit would remove his foot from my damn jugular.

"I SAID, LET HIM GO!" Jesuse demanded.

"He still hasn't told you yet, has he?" Biscuit asked.

"Told me what?"

"Looks like you two have some catching up to do!"

Finally, Biscuit removed his boot from my neck, and I fought to catch the air around me. He then ordered his hounds to back away, leaving me exposed and bleeding out on the ground. I could hear the sounds of them walking away through the crunching of the grass. Then suddenly, I saw him, Jesuse, bending over and extending out his hand. I was ashamed for him to see me in such a vulnerable state, and I pushed his hand away without thinking. He probably thought I was crazy for doing so, but I wanted to prove that I was strong enough to get up on my own. My body, however, didn't quite agree.

I COULDN'T understand why Josh would push my hand away after I saved his freaking life! I didn't have time for the theatricals; I knew that we needed to leave quickly because if the sound of gunfire didn't alert the police, I was sure that the neighbors would.

"Come on, stop being a dick and put your fucking pride to the side. We got to get out of here!"

I reached out my hand once more, and Josh stared at me long and hard before finally extending out his right hand. He looked terrible. I wasn't even sure if he had the strength to walk, but I had to try. After helping Josh off the ground, I let him lean into me as I walked him down the street to Ms. Bailey's house. And on the way, I periodically asked if he was okay or needed a break. He would just say,

"No…keep going…"

Even beaten and bruised, he was still a pain in the ass. When we finally made it to the house, I helped Josh into the bathroom and tried to get him cleaned up. But he had too much pride and prejudice to allow me to do much of anything. While he sat on the toilet, I grabbed a washrag and went to the kitchen for ice. When I returned, I gave the rag to Josh to lay it over his wounds. Josh then looked at me and said,

"This doesn't change anything between us. I still hate your fucking guts."

"Yeah, well, I'm not your biggest fan either. But I don't care about that shit right now. Biscuit almost killed your ass. But I guess you still plan on kissing his for the rest of the school year?"

"What's that supposed to mean? I don't kiss nobody's ass!"

"Whatever…"

I took a look at Josh's wounds, tried poking him gently on his ribs, and he hollered out like a wild hyena!

"I think you need to go to the hospital. You might have some broken bones."

"No, fuck that. I'm not going to the hospital. I'll call Crystal to come and get me."

I watched while Josh tried reaching for his phone inside his back pocket. He struggled even to see the dial pad. Finally, I snatched the phone, searched for Crystal's name, and dialed her number. After speaking to Crystal, I found out that she was still at school. When I told her what happened to Josh, she rushed right over. Not even ten minutes had passed before Crystal showed up dramatically banging on the door. I went to the living room and invited her inside. Josh was still sitting on the toilet when I walked Crystal into the bathroom. The look on her face was painful for even me to see.

"Oh my God...Josh, what the hell happened? Did Biscuit do this? I swear that asshole needs some serious..."

"I'm alright, Crystal. Can you take me to my car? I need to drive home."

"Like hell you will! Look at yourself, Josh! You're in no condition to be driving anywhere. You need to let me take you to the hospital."

"No...I don't want to go to the fucking the hospital. I'll be fine. Please, Crystal."

There was no reasoning with him. Josh was determined to do things the hard way.

"Listen to me...I can't just leave my car parked in the school parking lot for the next three weeks."

"Fine then! I'll drive you in your car and take you home. Then your parents can take you to the hospital!" I replied.

"No offense, but you're still banned from my house, not to mention the neighborhood. Just give me a minute to catch my breath, and I'll be okay. But, Jesus fucking Christ, it hurts to breathe!"

"That's why you need to stop being a stubborn ignoramus and let me take you to the hospital!" Crystal replied.

"I just need to rest... I'll be fine."

"No, you won't be fine if you have a concussion!" Crystal barked.

Crystal took the ice rag from Josh and dampened it around his face, cleaning up any blood she saw. So much was happening that I didn't even have time to process my feelings. Not until I was standing there in the bathroom watching

Crystal pampering Josh like a baby. And although his eyes were swollen and red, I could see the love he had for Crystal through her eyes. Right then was when I knew that Crystal and Josh had an unbreakable bond. It was probably silly to think about at that moment, but the mind can't help how it wanders. Then not even five minutes later, I heard Melanie and Ms. Bailey walking through the front door. I ran out of the bathroom to try and explain the situation before they flipped.

As I made my way down the hall, Melanie and Ms. B met me halfway and immediately, they both focused their attention on the bathroom behind me. And in the bathroom was a large mirror that faced the hallway, and from the hallway, you could see Crystal inside. The look on Melanie's face was priceless, and Ms. Bailey quickly became anxious as she stared back and forth between Crystal and me. Melanie then blurted out,

"Wow! You've got to be kidding me! Wait a minute, is that Josh in there too?"

Melanie then brushed past me and poked her head in the bathroom. After furiously shaking her head, Melanie turned back towards us, looked directly at Ms. Bailey, and said,

"You know if you buy a couple of tents and set them up outback, you might have enough room here for our entire senior class!"

"MELANIE!" Ms. Bailey shouted.

I could tell that Ms. B was becoming fed up. Melanie just brushed by the two of us and went upstairs. Ms. B then rushed inside the bathroom and gasped with,

"Oh…my goodness! Josh?"

"Hi, Ms. Bailey, you have a nice home, from what I'm able to see."

"Josh… Crystal, I don't know what happened, but you need to get this boy to a hospital now! Or call his parents so that they can take him! I'm sorry, Josh, but I cannot have you blending all over my house."

"I promise we'll go…I just needed to catch my breath, please. I don't want to go to a hospital." Josh replied.

"Your clothes are filthy and covered in blood! Jesuse, go in the garage. I have some spare clothes in a blue container next to the icebox."

"No…I don't want…"

"And don't even think about finishing that sentence. I don't care to hear about what you do or don't want to do. I will not be responsible should anything happen to you. We already lost one student this year to violence. You're going to a hospital, and that's final! Now, Crystal, are you going to call his parents, or shall I?"

Then after taking a look in the mirror, Ms. Bailey noticed me still standing behind her and said,

"Jesuse? Are you going to get the clothes?"

I immediately rushed to the garage to find clean clothes that Josh could change into. Ms. Bailey had so much junk in there that it was difficult for me to move around. She had many different containers with labels and even a pool table covered with old newspapers and boxes. No wonder her home looked so clean and free of clutter; her garage was her junk organizer. Curiosity got the best of me as I began snooping and wondering who the items in her garage belonged to. Ms. Bailey didn't strike me as the pool playing type, or maybe she was, and it was my own biases making up false conclusions. After spending another five minutes in the junkyard, I heard Ms. Bailey shouting my name.

I then grabbed a white t-shirt, black sweats and wiggled my way out of the garage and back into the bathroom. I sat the clothes on the counter next to the sink, and Crystal stayed in the bathroom to help Josh change. After Ms. Bailey and I walked into the hallway, she told me that Josh's dad was on his way. That's when I knew it was time to hightail it out of there. You know, with me still being on his family's most wanted list, I figured my face would be the last face his dad would want to see. But ironically, that selfish act of stealing is what helped me to save Josh from that prick. I believed that in some sick and twisted way, Biscuit got off on torturing people.

As Ms. Bailey and I made our way to the living room, I was almost ready to leave until I bumped into Melanie. She had her backpack and headphones on, ready to dip out too, I guess. But Ms. Bailey had a few words for both of us.

"Wait a minute, where are you both going?"

"I was just going to walk to the gas station, if that's okay?" I replied.

"Well, the next time you get the idea to sneak one of your classmates into my house dripping blood, use the back door. You got traces of bloodstains all over my white carpet, and now I'm going to need you to scrub every last one of them out!"

"Yes, ma'am...I apologize..."

"Mmhm...go on!" Ms. Bailey replied.

As I made my way towards the front door, I heard Melanie hurrying behind until Ms. Bailey sternly said,

"Wait, Melanie! You and I need to have a serious talk about this new attitude of yours!"

Ouch! I was very grateful that I wasn't in Melanie's shoes as I slid through the front door. Though I honestly didn't want to be in my shoes either. Especially with what happened to me earlier. I called myself trying to exterminate a problem when I ended up just spreading the fire. My day started after I got Ms. Bailey's car from school. It was still early in the morning when I made my way to Fernando's warehouse. It was vital for me to get there right before he left to run his errands. When I first started hustling for Fernando, he'd sometimes take me out with him while he'd take care of his business. Fernando didn't go out without at least two pushers. He had a loyal army of people working for him, with each person assigned a specific job. If Fernando wasn't flipping packs of molly and trees, then he was cleaning money.

So, when I arrived, I parked a block away diagonal from the building. And from there, I was able to see the people entering and exiting while also having a clear view of the alleyway. All I needed to do was wait and be ready for whenever Fernando made his way through in his white Yukon Denali. While sitting and waiting for over forty minutes, I noticed someone walking towards me. I couldn't make him out at first, but as he got closer, my heart began to pound hard and deep, for I was sure I had blown my cover. Then when I could finally make out his face, I exhaled from relief, knowing it was just Manny. This dude was about five foot seven, calm, and he never let his hair grow out more than an inch. So as

Manny got closer, I rolled down the window and waited for him to say,

"Yo, Jesuse? What are you doing out here, man? And is this you? Where'd you find the money to buy some new wheels?"

"It's not mine; I'm borrowing it!"

I tried to stay emotionless. Then without thinking, I placed my hand on the gun beside me and saw as Manny's eyes moved down to my hand, then back up at me.

"Are you borrowing that too?"

I didn't respond. I just stared ahead, with my attention focused on the ally, waiting for that white Yukon Denali to pull out. Then Manny went on to say,

"I know what you're doing out here...with that gun. Fernando's not dumb. He's praying that you show up and try something so that he can have a reason to take you out. I'm sorry about what happened to your mom. It wasn't right. But with Fernando, whether your fuck up is big or small, he delivers justice the same to make a point, and that is that nobody fucks with Fernando!"

"Yeah, well, I think it's time for people to realize that I'm the one not to be fucked with it."

Manny shook his head as he looked at me then back at the warehouse. After another couple of seconds, Manny looked back at me and said,

"If anyone asks, you didn't hear this from me. A few of the guys are in talks about switching sides. They don't necessarily like the way Fernando handles his business, especially after what happened to you. I have an address for you. I want you to go there. It will be someone there who can help you out!"

Manny discreetly handed me a business card, and on it read, *Katsumi Nails and Spa*, with an address and phone number on the bottom. I was stumped. I didn't know if he was setting me up or trying to help.

"Who the hell is going to help me with my problem at a nail shop? Is this a joke?"

"No, man, I'm for real. Just go there, and you'll see. Oh and, you'll need the password to get in."

"Really? And what's that?"

I leaned forward in anticipation to hear what Manny would say. Part of me believed I was being set up. I thought I'd drive to this nail shop, spa, or whatever, and meet my end. After being told the secrete word, I waited for Manny to walk away before I even considered driving to the address. I thought that if I just waited a bit longer, I could catch Fernando. But who was I kidding? Fernando was never alone, at least not in the public eye. I knew that if I were to catch Fernando, I would need a little bit of help. So, I decided to drive to the nail shop. I knew Manny, he was a good guy, and in the end, I didn't think he'd set me up to fall. I prayed at least that he wouldn't on my twenty-minute drive to the Northside of town. And when I got there, I was surprised by what I saw.

The nail shop was reasonably small. It stood alone like it was on its own island from the rest of the businesses. This part of town was also less crowded; the buildings were spread apart with lots of land in between. The snow was barely sticking to the ground. There was just enough for me to see a small sheet of it spread across the green grass. I parked to the side of the building. It was barely 10:30 A.M. when I arrived, and I could only see a couple of cars in the parking lot. After making my way inside, someone by the name of, Iris greeted me. This lady had long pink hair and wore a black apron with dark blue jean pants. I was confused; I didn't know what to say or do. She just looked at me and asked,

"How can I help you?"

"I don't know. Someone gave me a card with this address on it. I don't even know who I'm looking for, only that Manny told me to come here."

"Well, I'm the only person here right now, and I don't know you. We don't open until 10:30 A.M. You can come back later when we get busy; we'll have more people here who could probably assist you."

Iris then walked to one of the chairs, looked like she was getting things set up for a possible customer. I didn't want to have to leave, not after driving almost thirty minutes to get there, so I walked towards her and blurted out,

"I HAVE TINY SWEATY BALLS!"

"Excuse me?"

"Sweaty... Balls?"

Iris just glared at me as if I was the world's biggest idiot. Immediately I became frustrated and wondered, *how could Manny fucking set me up?* Then as I started to turn around and shamefully walk out of the building, a tall, clean-shaven bald guy wearing all back approached me.

"You're Jesuse?"

"Yeah?"

"Follow me..."

I followed Mr. Clean to the back of the shop, through the

swinging door, past the storage room, and to an elevator. *An elevator?* What the heck is an elevator doing in the back of a nail shop? I knew it couldn't go up; the building was only one story. What I hadn't considered, as I stepped inside and stood behind Mr. Muscle, was that the elevator wasn't going up but rather down. Okay, here's when my heart really started to pound. We stood quietly on the elevator for a good minute before we hit the bottom. I felt like I was inside of a James Bond film or part of the SAW collection. Right as I stepped out of the elevator, I prayed that Billy the puppet wouldn't be waiting for me on his tricycle.

The place did have that creepy vibe to it. The area was large, with tables neatly stacked in rows with small, medium, and large boxes on the tops. *What the hell is this place?* I asked myself. Then suddenly, I noticed a small room guarded by a metal fence. Inside the fence was a table and two chairs. After being ordered by Mr. Clean's muscles and dilated pupils to walk inside and take a seat, shit got real when he walked back out and locked me inside!

I was trying not to panic, but my heart was beating louder than the sound of horses on a racetrack. I just knew I was being set up. Of course, I was! Fernando wouldn't let me go that easily. He knew I'd do one of two things; try to kill his ass myself or run to the police. FUCK, I shouted. I gave up; I was ready to surrender. The entire time I sat there shaking my knees and twiddling my thumbs, I was succumbing with regret. I felt like a complete idiot for believing a word that Manny had said. Then after taking a few more deep breaths, inhaling and exhaling, I was shocked by the sound of a high-pitched whisper and the smell of lavender as I turned around and listened to the voice say,

"Jesuse, I'm so glad to finally meet you. Manny gave me the heads up that you'd be stopping by."

It was a WOMAN! A tall, mysterious, fashionably dressed, not to mention sexy, woman who unlocked the gate and walked inside! Then after entrapping me with her scent, the woman walked past me and sat on top of the desk. While facing me with a giant smile, I blurted out in confusion,

"I'm sorry but, who are you? And how do you know Manny?"

"Oh, Fernando didn't teach you the number one rule about asking questions?"

"N-no... what's the rule?"

"The rule is, DON'T! And I'm not here to answer your questions. But you are here to answer mine!"

"Uhm, okay..."

"I have a proposition for you."

Between this lady and Mr. Clean ogling me from behind, I didn't know what to think. Moments later, I watched as she slowly hopped off the desk, grabbed the other chair, and met me at eye level as she sat down.

"I'm sure you've heard this enough, but I'm going to say it anyway... I'm sorry for your loss. There's not a single person on the streets who doesn't know about what happened to you. Fernando might not be able to admit it to himself right now, but he fucked up, and people are starting to see it. Killing you, eh, it might have been a better solution, but your mother? Now that was beyond fucked up!"

"Why are you telling me this? What do you want?"

"Me? I want to help, Jesuse. I want to help you get your revenge! That's what you want, isn't it? I mean, I assume that's why you've been biking and car stalking Fernando around town?"

I was shocked. How did this woman know? I asked myself. And if she knew, a total stranger, I was positive that Fernando was more than aware of my tactics.

"Don't look so surprised, Jesuse. And yes, Fernando is well aware of what you've been up to. But that's Fernando; he will always be two steps ahead. He might be a messy son of a bitch, but he's also a smart son of bitch. And if you plan on successfully taking him out, you're going to need my help."

"You help? Why? What's in it for you? I know that people don't just do things out of the kindness of their hearts without wanting something in return. So what do you want?"

"Well, Jesuse, you are sadly right about that. Relationships are transactional. So, I guess I might as well just get right to the point! Jesuse, you're an asset in this community. And, I need someone like you on my side, working for me. You take care of mama, and she'll take care of you."

"WHAT?"

"Jesuse, let me be frank. You're never going to catch Fernando, not on your own. The only way and I do mean the only way you will catch him, is when he's ready to grind your bones into soup. You need me!"

"No! I don't need anybody! Dealing is what got my mom killed in the first place. I'm never getting myself involved in that shit again, ever! Find someone else. I can and will take care of Fernando on my own!"

"What do you think will happen to you when Fernando's

crew finds his body in an alley or buried underneath rubbish in the woods? Do you think everyone will forget and that life will go back to normal for you? That you'll be able to walk around here, free? Jesuse, you will never be free. You will spend the rest of your life running and hiding with a target on your back because no matter where you go, there will be someone there waiting to put a bullet through your skull. But, if you work for me, you'll have my full protection. You'll more than get the justice you deserve, but you'll also have your freedom. The choice is yours, and yes, you do have a choice. But Jesuse, if I were you, I'd make the right one, and quickly!"

And at that moment, without realizing it, I traded in my soul for freedom. I promised myself and my mom that I'd never get back into the business. Still, if I needed to get my hands dirty for a little while to even the score, then that's just what I was going to do.

While replaying the day in my head on my walk back to Ms. Bailey's, I knew I'd have to play things a lot smoother if I were to have any success in catching Fernando. When I made my way back through the front door, I noticed that Ms. Bailey had a bucket of soap water and a green scrubber placed in front of the kitchen doorway. Yeah, I almost forgot that I had another mess to clean up. However, I was thankful that Josh and Crystal were out of sight by the time I got back. And Melanie was either being occupied by one of her lovers or asleep upstairs. Whatever the case, the house was quiet, and that's exactly what I needed to think in peace. I felt terrible for not having any consideration of Ms. Bailey's home as I let

Josh bleed all over her carpet. But she was a saint for not kicking me out right then and there.

I spent the rest of the night scrubbing out the stains until I was sure the bloodstains were no longer visible. I then relieved myself of clean-up duty and headed to bed. I was so focused on the Fernando bullshit that I didn't even get the chance to spread my mother's ashes over the river. I felt terrible for lying to Ms. B because not only was I hiding one secret, but two. There were two delicate items that I kept hidden out of sight; the silver urn, which held my mother's ashes, and my new stash of molly. I only prayed, which I've grown to do a lot of recently, that my transgressions wouldn't catch up to me. The only question I had left was, how the hell would I sell 200 pills in a week, but more importantly, to who?

| 8 |

THE WAKE

IT WAS officially Saturday. I spent the entire week dreading this exact moment, second by second, as I slid into my super skinny ankle black slacks, deep grey button-up blouse, and my four-inch black high heels. It was 2 p.m. when I finally made my way downstairs for a cool glass of ice water to calm my nerves. And honey, my nerves were through the roof! I even kept my make-up light with just a little bit of black eyeliner, eye shadow, and a pop of shiny lip-gloss. Now, I probably wasn't dressed to kill it on *America's Next Top Model,* but I was confident that I would be the sexiest thing in any room I stepped into!

My mom and dad were downstairs in the kitchen, standing by the refrigerator eating a snack when I strutted my way towards them. I could tell they were eyeing me from the side, curious about what I was or wasn't wearing. Then my dad, out of the blue, said,

"No dress today? What?"

"Dad, I don't wear a dress every day. Only on certain special occasions."

"Well, isn't this a certain, special occasion?"

I despised it when my parents questioned my choice of clothing. As if I was only supposed to dress one way or the other. I felt like a free-spirited individual, and I never limited my form of expression based on what my gender or sexuality suggested. Then my mother said,

"Toni, you know that I don't have a problem with what you choose to wear day in and day out. But I do get confused sometimes. I mean, are you gay, a transvestite, transexual, or?"

"MOM?" I shouted.

"Honey, we love and support you as you are, you know that. But I have no idea what to say to people when they ask who my son is. Are you confused?" She asked.

"No, I'm not confused! And, when people ask you who I am, tell them I am Toni Broussard, eclectic, child of the universe, humble and kind. Anything beyond that...is not a factor!"

I loved how my parents tried so hard to support me, even though they didn't quite understand me. I just never thought I'd have to explain myself, who I am, to my parents. And honestly, most days, I wasn't sure of who I was either. I hated living in a world where one needed to fit into a box to be received as accepted. But, what if, as Gabrielle said, there wasn't a categorized box for me to slide into? What if I was just a blend of both worlds?

I didn't want to let those thoughts deter me from the afternoon ahead. Thankfully, my parents were able to drive me to Mrs. Bernard's house for James's wake. When we arrived, my jaw dropped by the number of cars that surrounded the driveway and street. As I walked inside and noticed a few familiar faces, it became more evident that the entire school got an invite. Well, I guess when you live in a home that equals the size of three, a crowd would be the least of your concern. So many people were huddled up in small groups, either sobbing, laughing, or sharing old stories with glasses of water in their hands.

I found a spot near the corner, thinking I could free myself of the chaos, and quietly morn. But the quiet never lasts for long, not in this town. So while my parents mingled with the other parents, my quiet, empty bubble expanded after Melanie, Renee, and Gabrielle entered the room. I put on a smile and anticipated the conversation to come.

"Toni! Oh my God, are you okay?" Gabrielle asked as she reached for a hug.

"Yes! I'm just so surprised to see everyone here!"

After inhaling Gabrielle's warm embrace, Melanie said,

"Well, of course, we're all here. The entire school is still trying to figure out which one of us killed James!"

"Melanie!" Gabrielle whispered.

"What? Look, I'm sorry, but I mean, over half the people in here didn't even know that James existed until last week."

"Girl, that may be true, but you know that times like these are what brings people together," Renee replied.

"Trust me. No one is coming together over James's death!" Melanie replied.

"Okay, well, there are some of us here who would like to pay our respects. So, with all due respect, Melanie, please show some!"

I love my girls, but I had to walk away before I caused a

scene. I just didn't understand why some people couldn't set their anger or pride to the side, even for the deceased. And just looking around the room, I could see that everyone was just trying to put on a good face. That they were staying long enough to make their appearance noted before cutting out. It was like a revolving door of empty emotions. It made me sick! Then after walking into the dining room area, I glanced at the photos displayed all over the room. It must have been fifty photos of James just spread out everywhere. I found myself daydreaming about what James was like as a kid. Finally, one picture stuck out to me; it was of James on a bike wearing a yellow t-shirt and blue jean shorts. He looked so happy in this photo; I couldn't help but smile to myself.

Before I could even reach to pick up the picture in the frame, I heard a voice. It was a deep, sexy, baritone, chocolaty, 5 foot 11 inches of handsome that startled me by saying,

"Excuse me! I don't mean to startle you. My name is Michael. I'm an old friend of James."

Oh my God, thee Michael? I couldn't think of what to say. I was standing in front of my deceased lover's ex! And how he introduced himself as an *old friend*, please! I knew who you were, Michael! Though I tried to play it cool, after choking over my words when I finally came to and said,

"Hi, Michael, I know who you are!"

As Michael and I were shaking hands, I checked out his front, and he was checking out my back. The chemistry was unreal, but I had to snap out of it and remember just who Michael was. Oh, but I couldn't help myself! He was just too gorgeous; I became hypnotized! Then I began feeling like a hypocrite. There I was, craving this dashing dark chocolate while standing two feet away from James's casket!

"So tell me, old friend of James's, how deep did your friendship go?"

"We were pretty close...we dated. Which I'm guessing you somehow already figured that out."

"Yes, James told me a lot about you."

"Mostly good things, I hope?"

"No... not at all!" I replied while folding my arms.

"Well, can you see now why I didn't open with; *Hi, I'm James's ex*, especially given the circumstances?"

"What circumstances?" I asked in confusion.

"Well, take a look around. We aren't exactly meeting at a party. And also, most people who knew of James's and I's relationship know that it wasn't exactly the healthiest."

I slowly walked further into the dining room, staring at James's photos, and Michael followed behind.

"Listen, I don't know you or what happened in the past. I just know how you affected his present." I replied.

"And I don't know what James may have told you about me, but he was no saint! Last week, actually, the day of the dance, he was blowing up my phone, begging me to take him back. You know, everyone here is acting like he was the victim, but James was no victim!"

"Oh, so you are? And what are you talking about? James wasn't even thinking about you. He was too busy begging me to take him back! You know what, you're a selfish snake! Standing here lying on the dead just to make yourself look better when we both know that you're the reason..."

I paused. I had to catch myself before I said it. After taking a moment to breathe and calm my nerves, I continued with,

"I know what you did to James, the way that you treated him. You destroyed him! Some people choose to remain ignorant about their actions instead of looking in the mirror and making a change. But, I won't allow you to disrespect James in his house while his body is in the other room. James wasn't a perfect person, but he at least tried to be in the end. Can you say the same for yourself, now?"

"I'm sorry if I...I didn't mean to offend you. But I won't lie to you or put on a fake smile like everyone else here. There are three sides to every story, and if you'd like to know my version and the truth, give me a call."

After grabbing the pen from his blazer, and a napkin from the coffee table, Michael quickly wrote down his number. Of course, I didn't want it! And when Michael tried to hand me the napkin, I just looked at him like he was crazy. Finally, after realizing that my hands weren't going to budge from my side, he placed the napkin down on the coffee table and walked away with a smirk. Michael knew he got under my skin, and he also knew that he was charming as fuck! So, while I stood alone contemplating to myself and replaying the conversation in my head, I made sure that Michael was out of sight before I snatched the napkin with his number written in blue ink. After making my way back to the living room, I waited to be greeted by Melanie and Gabrielle.

"Hey, I'm sorry for being insensitive earlier. I just have a lot of crap that I'm still dealing with. Can you ever forgive the error of my ways?" Melanie asked.

I could tell that Melanie was sincere even through her humor. So I smiled, embraced her with a tight hug, and reassured her that all was forgiven.

"So, you two seem to be doing better. I'm assuming you finally solved the dilemma in your relationship?" I asked.

Melanie looked timid like she wasn't quite sure of what to say. Then Gabrielle quickly jumped in and said,

"Well, we're still working on things. But yes, I think we're finally sorting through the kinks!"

I watched the two of them; their body language, and I could immediately tell Melanie was holding back. I couldn't get into their drama, not at the wake, but I made sure to take note and pack it into memory to address at another time. I then looked over to my left and noticed that Renee was in the living room corner talking to Jesuse. I didn't even know that Jesuse was there! I figured he must have shown up while I was being distracted by Michael and his chocolate drizzle. Speaking of Michael, he seemed to have just disappeared right after our conversation. I looked around the room, peeked into the kitchen, but nothing, he was gone. Then as soon as I glanced back over at Jesuse and Renee, I was baffled when I saw Josh and the gang dramatically walking through the front door.

Josh looked like Hannibal Lecter on his worst day with bandages all over his face and chin, not to mention, he could barely walk. It took Crystal and Josh's parents to help escort him inside. I turned back to Melanie and Gabrielle and said,

"Oh my! What happened to Josh?"

"I'm still trying to figure that one out," Melanie replied.

"What do you mean? Honey, please empty your teacup!"

"Really, Toni? My teacup?" Melanie sighed.

"Just hurry up and spill the tea before I pee on myself!"

"I don't know anything. All I know is that when I got home, Josh was sitting on the toilet with blood oozing out from everywhere while Crystal and Jesuse tended to his every need!"

"Wait, wait, wait…wait a minute! Josh and Jesuse, in the same room, together, and at your house?"

"You mean, Ms. Bailey's Orphanage? I mean, excuse me, sorry! I forget that I'm supposed to be working on my attitude. And that I need to appreciate all the love and support I have. Oh, and that there's nothing wrong with sharing!"

Gabrielle and I both stared at each other, dumbfounded by Melanie's comment. Then Gabrielle said,

"I'm confused. Did Jesuse do that to Josh? But wait, that wouldn't make any sense if they were both at your house?"

"Exactly! Besides, they've been fighting since freshman year, and Josh almost always walks away with barely a scratch. Well, except for last week when Jesuse pulverized his face. But no, whoever did this to Josh was smarter, much stronger, and…oh, of course…"

"Of course, what, honey?" I asked.

I followed Melanie's eyes as she glared over at the front door. Josh and the gang were making their way around the room when Biscuit, and his WWE twin father, barged their way inside. Immediately, I looked over to see if Josh noticed, as he was only a couple of feet away from Biscuit. But when Josh finally turned his head towards the front door, after screaming in agony, the look in his eyes when he saw Biscuit was priceless. I'd never seen Josh look so petrified. He tried to play it cool by limping over to a nearby chair and taking a seat. Melanie, Gabrielle, and I quietly walked closer only to snoop, and Renee and Jesuse quickly followed suit. It seemed as if everyone could smell the smoke in the air, and Renee then whispered,

"You guys, it's about to get real up in here!"

"Okay, I need somebody to spill the damn tea!" I whispered back.

Before Jesuse could open his mouth, the room became quiet, too quiet. Biscuit and Gravy slowly approached Josh and the gang while everyone else in the room was anxiously waiting to see what would happen. I could sense that the breakfast surprise sent Josh's dad into a frenzy, yet he held his composure until given a chance to speak.

"Excuse me, Mr. Fleming? I figured we'd come by to offer our sympathies personally. But, sadly, there are just some people in this world who have to learn life lessons the more physical way, if you catch my drift," Biscuit's dad replied before winking at Josh.

Biscuit stood close, quietly smirking while shaking his head in amusement. Mr. Fleming then went on to say,

"The only thing I'm going to catch is a case if you two don't get the hell away from my son! Your boy is lucky that we didn't press charges. But I swear, if that animal lays another finger on my son, I will personally see to it that his body becomes one with a motorized wheelchair. If you catch *my* drift!"

"Is that a threat Mr. Fleming?"

"Oh, it's a promise!"

The two stood face-to-face, inches away with their chests

pumped and ready to swing a punch. My dad then came to the rescue, standing in front of them, and quietly said,

"Gentlemen! We are guests in this house for the sole purpose of paying our respects to Mrs. Bernard and her family. So whatever drama you two have going on, leave it at the door. We're at a awake, not a damn cage fight!"

"And who are you? Oh wait, I know… you're the father of the sexually confused. My deepest sympathies, truly. But why don't you step aside and let us real men talk while you go help your son reapply his lipstick." Biscuit's dad replied.

There wasn't even a pause or moment of hesitation before my dad went to grab Biscuit's father by the collar with his fists, clenching tightly exposing his veins. I couldn't let my dad get dragged down to hell with them, so I had to intervene.

"Dad, please, let him go!"

Before my dad released his hold, Mrs. Bernard startled everyone as she came running into the living room troubled and confused. And as soon as she laid eyes on Biscuit, her face went from hot orange to deep red!

"What the hell is going on in here? And you, what are you doing in my house? You are not welcome here. Get out! NOW!"

Mrs. Bernard pointed to the door as she waited for Biscuit and his father to walk out. But Biscuit wasn't going to leave without getting the last word.

"Mrs. Bernard, I truly am sorry for your loss. I only wanted to pay my respects. But you're angry with the wrong person. I do hope you find James's killer! Well, enjoy the rest of your evening!"

Biscuit smiled so condescendingly as he and his dad walked past Mrs. Bernard on their way out. Mrs. Bernard then looked to the rest of us in the room and said,

"If anyone else here has intentions other than mourning the death of my son, you can follow your asses right behind them! My world was torn completely apart. And you all are just standing around here arguing, fighting, or laughing about things that have nothing to do with my son. I am suffering, and…"

"Mrs. Bernard, please allow me to apologize. For a brief second, I allowed another man's ignorance to cloud my judgment and distract me from the reason we're all here in the first place. But, I promise you, my family and I, we are only here for you and your family and to pay our respects."

Well, all right, dad! I was so proud! Then Mr. Fleming went on to say,

"Same here! And if you'll still have us, we promise that we will pay our respects and be out of your way."

The room stood quiet as everyone waited for Mrs. Bernard's reply. Then after a few seconds, she wiped her tears and walked back into the dining room. The room then slowly filled up with vibrations of chatter. I watched as Jesuse approached a couple of the guys from our school who were standing near James's casket. And honey, was I baffled when I saw Jesuse reach into his pocket and slip both of them a small white prize. I had to approach and confront him!

"What the hell, Jesuse? So you're back to doing this shit again? And what is that anyway, Heroin?"

"Toni, shh! And calm down, it's not what you think!"

"Oh really? Because I think it's exactly what I think. You're using James's wake as an opportunity to sell drugs?"

"I can't get into this with you right now, please. Just, promise you won't say anything?"

"Ugh, my God! I can't with you right now. I just can't!"

I was seconds away from slapping the living daylights out of him. I wanted to so badly! But the good in me took over, and I peacefully stormed away while passing Josh and Crystal on the way to the restroom; I just needed to clear my mind.

WOAH! Toni bolted out of the living room so fast that I didn't even get a chance to utter the word, hello. However, it could have also been because I could barely breathe, move a muscle, or cartilage to raise my hand. I asked Crystal to help me out of the chair while my parents were mingling. I wanted to speak to Jesuse and let him know that I appreciated what he did for me even though I still couldn't stand his ass. After tiptoeing my way across the room with Crystal's help, I got Jesuse's attention by saying,

"Hey! I just wanted to say thank you for saving my life. I owe you one!"

"It was nothing. I'm sure you would have done the same for me!"

"Well…"

"It's okay! I wasn't expecting us to become best friends or anything. I just did what any other person with a beating heart would have done."

"Hey! I have a heart! Why do you people keep saying that? Although right now, it feels like it's about to drop into my ass!"

While I was trying to make light of the situation, my dad approached with my mom following shortly behind.

"I want to thank you for saving my son's life. You could have turned the other cheek, but instead, you went and earned your place in this country as a true American citizen. That's what we do around here. We take care of one another!"

Earned your place in this country? Even I was surprised when I heard those words come out of my dad's mouth. But, I was in too much pain to argue with him, so I let my dad continue embarrassing me by adding,

"I still have one tiny problem, though, Jesuse, one that I can't seem to solve. Do you remember the day that you broke into my house like some loose raccoon and stole from my wife?"

"You mean, ex-wife!" My mom interrupted.

"Sure, honey, whatever you say! As I was saying, my *wife* is missing a bracelet, one that I bought for her 40th birthday. You wouldn't happen to have run across it while you were in our bedroom digging for gold, would you?"

"No, sir, I don't remember seeing a bracelet. And, again, I apologize for breaking into your house."

"It's fine, son... I just thought I'd ask. And I'm terribly sorry for your loss as well!"

That was the shortest and most uncomfortable conversation of the night. I could tell that my dad was skeptical, that he didn't quite believe Jesuse. But because Jesuse saved me from becoming a pile of broken bones, all was forgiven. After Jesuse awkwardly walked away, I felt the urge to step outside and get some fresh air. It was becoming way too stuffy inside, and I didn't know if it was my guilt resurfacing or the crowd of people in the house, but I knew I needed to get out. I had Crystal escort me outside, and she sat with me on the ledge out front. I could tell that her mind was wandering because she does this thing with her nose when she wants to ask me something but doesn't quite know what to say. So, I went ahead and asked,

"What is it, Crystal?"

"What do you mean?"

"How long has it been now, six years? I know you almost better than I know myself. You clearly have something on your mind. What is it?"

"I don't...I just...how did we end up here? I mean, look at you. We were good people. You used to be a good person. I never imaged that you'd get involved with a person like Biscuit."

"So, just to be clear, you're saying I'm a bad person now? And exactly what kind of bad are we talking here, Michael Jackson BAD or?"

"I'm serious, Josh! Are you ever going to tell me what you were doing at Jesuse's house that night?

And we were back to that question again. To be honest, it was giving me stress diarrhea.

"And you know what the sad thing is... I'm already 99.9% sure of what the truth is. I just need you to say it..." Crystal begged.

"Do you remember when we were kids, seventh grade? We were total nerds: me and my high waters and you with your huge round glasses and Power Puff girl backpacks. We didn't have anyone else, but we had each other. And that was okay with me because I adored the hell out of you. I remember you'd be in class drawing up these wedding dresses and skirts. You were so talented, do you remember?"

"Oh my God, that feels like such a long time ago!"

"Why'd you stop?"

"I don't know, I just...I guess I didn't think I was really any good at it."

"Come on, Crystal! I even saved some of your drawings. I figured I'd keep them to remind your future self of who you are, but instead, I ended up being the one who needed reminding. The truth is that I'm confused. I'm lost and confused, and I have no idea why I've been trying so hard to prove myself worthy to someone who would, in the end, wind up beating the living shit out of me! This ass whopping, it uh, really woke me up to a new perspective on life. I see now how I let fear feed my insecurities, and how it drove me into doing some really fucked up shit."

"Fears about what?"

"My biggest fear was losing you, Crystal. And that ended up happening anyway. You don't understand how much you meant to me all these years, how much you still mean to me. I don't have to tell you what I was doing at Jesuse's house that night, you already know. And now, I have to spend every day living with regret knowing that I almost took an innocent life for reasons that make absolutely no sense. I promise, Crystal, I didn't do it, someone else got to Jesuse's mom first. And no, it wasn't Biscuit. The voice I heard in the house that night was... it was unfamiliar. Look, I'm sorry that I let you down. Trust me; I let myself down as well."

Then I felt it come over me, the emotions that I'd been harboring inside for days. As the tears squeezed through the corner of my swollen purple eye, I suddenly couldn't see. I tried to wipe them away, but more only dripped out.

"I'm sorry, you probably think I'm pathetic right now."

Without saying a word, I felt Crystal's hand gently brush against my cheek as she patted my tears away. Even though I could barely see, I saw enough to know that Crystal was showing me kindness and love with every reassuring touch. The complete opposite of what I thought she would do. Once my eyes were clear of teardrops, Crystal looked at me and said,

"I just hope that you'll be able to find a way to forgive yourself because living with that kind of guilt...it will tear you apart. And you didn't lose me, stop saying that. I don't think you could ever truly get rid of me. We may not be able to be together right now, and we may have had some pretty bad arguments recently, but when all the fighting is done, you are still my person, and I love you! I will always be there for you even when you're acting like a complete doofus."

There were no words to describe how I felt hearing her say that. I think I even cracked a smile.

"I should head back inside. Are you coming?" Crystal asked.

"Yeah, in a minute. I don't feel like moving just yet."

"Okay, well, just scream when you're ready to come back in."

"Alright... I'll be fine. Go ahead."

Sitting there on the ledge, I smiled as I watched Crystal walk back inside. It meant so much to hear her say that I was her person. Most days, I felt like she hated my guts. But when I was in dire need, Crystal reminded me of the true meaning of friendship. I didn't think that a person like me deserved it, especially after all the things I've said, the people I hurt, and for what? I couldn't think of a single reason that would have justified my actions. And the troubling part of it was realizing that the person I treated the worst ended up saving me from the person I admired for all the wrong reasons. Some judge of character I was. I realized that if I were going to be worthy of love and kindness, I needed to act in that and tell Jesuse the truth. I needed his forgiveness. But more importantly, I needed to figure out a way to forgive myself...

| 9 |

THE COURSE

LIFE HOLDS many lessons. Some lessons are abrupt, giving you the chance to adjust your state of mind while checking your karma quickly. Other lessons, however, linger in the darkness like growing mold attacking your soul. And if lucky, eventually, you'll get through the cloud of darkness and rise above stronger and wiser. Sadly, we don't always get to choose our path. More often, our path chooses us. And for me, my path took me down a road of endless destruction. It all began right before Christmas break. I found myself torn again between two loves. And I know you probably hate me right now for what I've done. But, please understand, people are not their mistakes, and life isn't as Black and White as you may think. Though if you'll allow, I'd like to explain.

So, I had every intention of telling Gabrielle the truth about my recent transgressions. I swear I did! In fact, after that awkward dinner with Lucifer himself, I had it in my mind that Gabrielle and I would never be able to be together. So, was I wrong for allowing myself to get sucked into Ms. Bloom's pretty flower? If you'd seen those eyes, how welcoming they were, how vulnerable and open she was, and after a night like what I had, wouldn't you have done the same? Well, as I stated before, I had every intention of coming clean, letting Gabrielle know that I felt it would be best if she and I went back to being just friends. But when I saw Gabrielle at school the next day in tears, begging for five minutes of my time, how could I say no?

We walked into the cafeteria and grabbed breakfast right before first period. As soon as we sat down, I did nothing but listen to Gabrielle apologizing for her father's actions and promising that she wouldn't let anything or anyone come between us. I felt so guilty. What could I say? *I'm sorry, Gabrielle, but while you were reclaiming your rights and fighting for our love, I was smothering myself in Ms. Bloom's pizza crust?* I couldn't do that to her. And when Gabrielle leaned across the table, staring at me with those wondrously sultry eyes, I couldn't pull away when her lips met mine for a soft and yet moist peck. The entire time, I had my one eye glued to the cafeteria door, praying Ms. Bloom wouldn't walk inside. And so that's how it happened. I found myself torn between Ms. Bloom, the passionate, attentive protector, and Gabrielle, the more sensitive, innocent, humble fighter. What was I to do?

I was stuck, more so at this point than ever before, because I didn't want to lose either one of them. And the stress it took to spend the rest of the day dividing my time and attention between reassurances and hidden kisses was mentally and emotionally draining. I was thankful that winter break was less than an hour away. I figured I'd have the whole mess sorted out by then, at least I hoped. And, when I wasn't living

out my life as Indiana's most eligible bachelorette, I was playing hide and seek with my mother. Only to get back home
and have to stare at Jesuse all day. I swear, if he wasn't mop-
ing around the house in his pajamas, then he was pumped
up on speed, or whatever the hell it was that had him going
nonstop. Oh, and the day when half of the drama club was in
our bathroom, and Ms. Bailey had enough of my negative re-
marks, she pulled me to the side and said,

*"I understand that you're unhappy with the living arrange-
ments right now, but that doesn't make it right for you to be disre-
spectful. I took you in out of the goodness of my heart, same with
Jesuse. It doesn't make me love or want you any less. But this new
attitude of yours, I don't like it at all. This isn't the person you were
raised to be, not by me. There's plenty of love to go around, Melanie.
Don't be so stingy. And besides, if you aren't happy here, you don't
have to stay. I don't want you to leave; please know that I don't, but
I'm not forcing you to stay either."*

I didn't know what to think after that conversation. Part
of me understood where Ms. Bailey was coming from, but
then there was that egotistical part of me that felt betrayed
and replaceable. Either way, I knew that I was out of line and
made sure that any ill feelings I had about Jesuse, I would
keep them to myself moving forward.

However, Christmas break proved to be a challenge. I
spent almost every day cooped up in the house preparing for
December 25th with Jesuse as we decorated the Christmas
tree inside and the house outside with lights. It felt like Ms.
Bailey was trying to force us into doing things together. I
even baked a couple of cakes with Jesuse annoyingly by my

side, handing me the cups of sugar. I had to be civil, though, because I knew that the alternative would have been spending the holidays at papa *Berenstain's* house with my mother. Even the days leading up to Christmas day were a challenge. I had to once again sneak and divide my time between Gabrielle and Ms. Bloom by slurping cups of hot cocoa with one and sliding under the mistletoe with the other. And by the time mid-February rolled around, I think that's when I finally summoned up the courage to come clean. I had to! My heart and my conscience couldn't continue the lie. So there I was, walking down the school halls of Lee Wallace High before first period ready to make my choice. But I was interrupted when I spotted Toni strutting down the hall. He had on a new rainbow-colored attitude, and I just had to ask,

"Well, well, well! So what is this I see? A new pair of skinny jeans? And is this a new scarf too? So what's gotten into you, or should I ask who?"

"Honey, you know I don't sex and tell!"

"Hm, okay! So, I see we're also finally out with the dead and in with the...Michael?"

"Okay, let's not go that far! I still have much respect for my late James. But Michael has been keeping me very distracted lately?"

"Evidently! Jeez, Toni."

"What! I just wanted the tea, honey! I had no idea it would turn into more. But I did find out that the story James told me about how Michael was this enormous cheater was a lie! Michael swore up and down that he was always faithful and that it was James who cheated on him!"

"Really? Well, why would James lie about that? And how do you know that Michael isn't just messing with you?"

"Because after hearing Michael's side of things and getting to know him..."

"And his penis!" I jokingly added.

"I found out that he's a really sweet guy!" Toni sternly replied.

"Well, Toni, I just hope you're not getting caught up in the fairytale of things. People can be excellent liars!"

"What's that supposed to mean?"

"It means that people will tell you what you need to hear just to get what they want from you. You should probably get to know his brain more and his penis a little less. Just saying..."

After giving me the side-eye, Toni and I continued walking and talking until we reached my locker. Right as I was ready to turn the nob on the lock, I was startled by Gabrielle as she rushed up from behind, throwing her arms around my neck, kissing me on the cheek. I FREAKED! The first thought I had was, *I hope Ms. Bloom didn't see.* I could tell I surprised Gabrielle with my cold response and hesitation as she said,

"Melanie, what's wrong? Why are you so jumpy?"

Without thinking, because I couldn't, I stumbled over my words and blamed my jumpiness on my mother. With my history, I was sure Gabrielle would understand. And I believed Gabrielle understood because she didn't ask any other questions. I just knew that I was in the clear, especially when Toni began distracting Gabrielle with the most exciting topic of the month, Michael! So while they were distracting one another with the conversation, I had become distracted by a black lace thong hanging inside my locker. SHIT! I was on the verge of a heart attack! Then as Toni and Gabrielle's voices started to fade, my mind began hallucinating the sounds of intense moaning coming from Ms. Bloom's mouth. I had to snap myself out of it. I slammed my locker shut, turned around, and Both Toni and Gabrielle were glaring at me in confusion.

"Honey, what's going on with you? And why are you look-ing like you just seen a ghost?" Toni asked.

"Because I did! A giant, black spider was uhm; it was hang-ing at the top of my locker. So yeah, I think I'll wait to switch out my books later. Oh, and you know what, speaking of books, I just remembered that I have Renee's science book in my backpack. So I'm going to find her and give it back to her before the bell rings. I'll see you guys later?"

I left Toni and Gabrielle standing in the hallway, speech-less. I felt terrible for lying to Gabrielle, but I needed to find Ms. Bloom and figure out why in the hell she would do such a thing. Was she trying to get us caught, or me, more so to the point? I didn't know what went through her head when she decided to break into my locker a leave behind her perfume-infused underwear. But I was ready to find out!

UNBELIEVABLE, the whole thing was just ridiculous! I knew exactly what was going on. I wasn't a fool. I smiled and pretended that I wasn't bothered when Melanie darted down the hall without so much as giving me any eye contact, a hug, or even a kiss on the cheek, goodbye. I was pissed! Extremely and utterly pissed! And then, when she made up that outrageous excuse for why she freaked out when I kissed her, I had to keep the steam of smoke from blowing out the side of my face! After I parted ways with Toni and headed to my first-period class, I was greeted by two of my friends along the way. I just wasn't at all in the mood for socializing. So while I pouted my way into my classroom and flopped down in my chair, I sat there in a daze analyzing Melanie and I's entire relationship.

I noticed things started to change during Christmas break. Melanie wasn't as affectionate or focused. It was like her mind was always somewhere else. At first, I thought Melanie was only distant because of what happened the night I invited her over for dinner. It just seemed like she was still bothered by the whole situation, even after we talked, which gave me terrible anxiety. I could never tell what Melanie was thinking. And when I'd asked, she would give me some lame excuse for her distant behavior. Even the last week of Christmas break, now that's when I could tell things were starting to change. It was one of the nights she invited me over, and both Ms. Bailey and Jesuse were gone. So we had the whole house to ourselves.

Melanie and I were upstairs in her room, listening to her radio. She had a mix CD playing old 90's slow jams. I watched from her bed as she stood by the dresser fidgeting with the nobs, and I waited for her to ask me to dance. But instead, Melanie just turned around and continued leaning against the dresser with an empty smile. It was awkward. It was as if we were back to being strangers who didn't know how to act around each other. I was growing bored of the silence. So, I decided to get up and make the first move by asking,

"Do you want to dance?"

"To this?" Melanie asked with confusion.

"Yes! Why not?" I laughed.

Nice and Slow was playing about halfway through. I grabbed Melanie by the hand and walked her to the middle of the room. I then gently took her arms and placed them around my waist while glaring deep into her eyes, waiting for her to pull me close. I was trying every move out of the book that I could remember. But Melanie only stood there, swaying from side to side like she barely wanted to touch me. I couldn't understand why she was still so distant. Melanie and I had barely kissed all winter break, and I was starting to feel like she no longer wanted me. So after gently pushing her away, I said,

"You know what, it's fine. We don't have to dance together, we don't have to kiss, and as a matter of fact, we don't even have to be together!"

I charged towards the door red-faced and confused. Melanie then chased after me, grabbed me by the arm, and begged me not to leave, but I was no longer in the mood to talk.

"Every time I try to touch you, you completely freak out! You haven't even tried to kiss me. The only time you'll kiss me is whenever I ask. What is that? I shouldn't have to ask you for affection! I sacrificed my relationship with my dad just to be with you. But if you don't want to be with me anymore, if you...if your heart is somewhere else, then tell me!"

"It's not! My heart is with you!"

"Then why does it not feel that way?"

"I'm sorry that I haven't been giving you what you need, what you deserve, lately. But I really am dealing with a lot. I was literally fighting with my mom not even a month ago. She treats me like two-week-old trash. It's no excuse, I know. I just need you to be patient with me, please."

I couldn't believe what I was hearing. And watching the tears run down Melanie's face was enough for me to open up my arms and let her back in. I felt terrible for being insensitive. And just like that, I took what she said at face value and ignored my gut. I guess that's what happens in relationships. You ignore the truth, your gut instinct because the lie is more comforting than the truth. It wasn't until we were back in school, walking the halls, that I knew something more was going on.

While sitting in my first-period class, I realized that I needed to face the one person I had been avoiding all year long. I needed to protect my relationship, at whatever costs. Once first period was finally over, I headed down the hall to find Ms. Bloom and confront her once and for all. When I finally made it to her classroom, I saw she was standing near her desk, looking like she was about to walk out. I could tell because she had her feet pointed towards the door while her body hung over the desk. After staring for five seconds, I took a deep breath, walked inside, and said,

"Excuse me, Ms. Bloom, can we talk for a minute?"

I could tell that I caught her by surprise. And the look of guilt displayed all over her face was enough to condemn her alone."

"S-sure, but let's make it quick. We only have about five minutes."

I was already on edge, annoyed by the whole situation. But when Ms. Bloom approached me like I was a menacing teen, I could no longer keep the bull inside of me, tamed.

"I don't know how to say this nicely but, if there is…whatever is going on, between you and Melanie, I think you should end it. We're together now, and whatever you two had, it's over!"

"Wow! You have a lot of nerve coming into my classroom making demands based solely on your insecurities."

"Excuse me?"

"You heard me! You're a child! And as a child, it's time that you learn your place here. The relationships that I build with my students are none of your business. Your only job here is showing up on time and doing the work that's assigned to you. You do not write my checks. You do not oversee my classes. You do nothing, and so you are nothing! And, if you're having an issue with a certain someone, put on your big girl panties and take it up with them! Now, if you'll excuse me, I was just on my way out!"

I didn't know what to say. The coldness and lack of heart Ms. Bloom showed was utterly mindboggling. I tried to hold my composure as I walked away, wiping off the small amounts of drool that had formed on the side of my mouth. And after being *put in my place*, the thought finally occurred to me. I had been searching for the truth in all the wrong places. And I decided, after walking back into the hall, that I would *put on my big girl panties* and finally force Melanie to tell me the truth.

When school was out for the day, I found Melanie by her locker, putting on her coat. We hadn't spoken much prior, not even during lunch. I went to have lunch with my friends because, for one, I hadn't seen much of them, and two, I wasn't cooled off enough to confront Melanie without causing a scene. I was surprised, though, that she didn't come over and ask me to sit with her. I could feel it in my gut that something was about to happen. And as I found myself by her locker, she glared at me with sad eyes and insisted that we should go to her house to talk without interruption, and so I agreed. We gently smiled at one another before walking down the hall and out of the building.

On our way to her house, I was shaking, not just from the cold air and sheets of ice and snow on the ground, but because I was a nervous wreck. My heart broke more and more with each step we took. I even got a case of the bubble guts, but I tried not to let her see it. Then suddenly, out of nowhere, Melanie grabbed me by the hand, and there we were, holding hands the rest of the way. It felt so good to have her initiate some kind of physical contact with me. I started to warm up inside, and I thought, maybe not knowing was better. Well, I felt like I already knew the truth, but I thought that maybe living in a world of assumption would be better than confirmation. But that was just fear talking. So I talked myself out of the nonsense and took a deep breath as we made it to the front door of her house.

When I followed Melanie inside, I quickly became confused by the voices I heard chattering in the room ahead. The voices were familiar. Melanie and I followed the voices until we saw the faces that matched those voices. And boy, were we surprised when we saw Jesuse, Josh, and Crystal standing around the dining room table *giggling*! The look on Melanie's face was hilarious as she stared long and hard before blurting out,

"Are you serious, Jesuse? Are you doing this just to piss me off?"

"Calm down, Melanie! Everything's not about you." Jesuse replied.

"No, I know it's not! But you keep forgetting that you don't live here. You're a guest. And guests do not invite other guests over to a house that they don't live in!"

"Well, that's where you're wrong. I do live here. But I didn't invite Josh and Crystal to stay."

"Well then, if you didn't, then who the hell did?"

"I DID!"

Melanie and I both turned around when Ms. Bailey approached us from behind. She was wearing a comfortable sweatshirt and black jeans. The five of us stood quietly around the dining room table, waiting to hear what else Ms. Bailey had to say.

"I invited them to stay!"

"Why! And what are you doing here so early?" Melanie asked.

"I had a doctor's appointment. I told you about this last week, Melanie."

"Okay, but why are they here?"

Before Ms. Bailey could reply, Josh interrupted and said,

"I was dropping Jesuse off when Ms. Bailey invited Crystal and me to stay for dinner."

"Dinner! Okay, is this some kind of punishment? Do you hate me now or something? Jesuse was one thing but, Josh? Do you know that he was standing in the hallway calling me a slave not even six months ago? That's what he thinks of us. That's what they think of us! And I don't understand why you keep trying to force me to be around Dr. Racist and Sr. Homophobic?"

"Melanie, I owe you an apology. I should never have called you that!" Josh interrupted.

"Oh, cut the fucking act! I'm not buying it!"

"Enough, Melanie! Uniting people because of their differences is not what's being forced here. But maybe the world would start to become a better place if it were, hmm? Now, I have greens in the sink, pork chops ready to be seasoned, along with macaroni and cheese and cornbread still to be made! Today, we are going to celebrate life and the true meaning of the word togetherness! So, let's enjoy the times we have left with one another and flourish in it!"

"Well, jeez, Ms. Bailey, you're not about to die on us, are you?" Josh asked jokingly.

"Josh, why would you ask that?" Crystal interrupted."

"I was just...I wasn't serious! I was Joking!"

"I told you he was an idiot," Melanie added.

"Okay, alright, that's enough! Now, who here is good with a knife? Crystal"

"I mean, I'm decent...but..."

"Great! Crystal and Gabrielle, come help me in the

kitchen! Jesuse, I want you to take Melanie and Josh to the garage and finish sorting through those donation boxes. I need to get half of the garage organized and boxed up by morning."

"Well, so much for freedom of choice!" Melanie replied.

And there we were, separated, for a cause we had yet to understand. I grew anxious as I followed Ms. Bailey and Crystal into the kitchen with high nerves. Nervous because that much-needed talk Melanie and I were supposed to have had gotten more and more delayed. But I took a calmer approach after washing my hands and preparing to clean greens for the first time. It was awkward at first, with Crystal standing just two feet away. She always seemed to have an attitude whenever I was around her. And extra attitude on top of mine was the last thing I needed. So I planned to keep to myself and not say a word. It wasn't until the house phone rang and Ms. Bailey walked into the living room that Crystal forced me to open my mouth.

"Hey, I know I've been acting like a bitch towards you lately; I'm sorry. I think we've all just been dealing with our own shit, you know?"

"Yeah, I can agree. With the school shooting, issues with my dad, and now Melanie. Especially Melanie! It just seems like we have a massive load of *shit* standing in between us lately."

"Oh, are you talking about, Ms. Bloom?"

"Huh! How do you...what do you know about Ms. Bloom?"

"Oh, shit. I thought you... I don't want to get involved. I'm not even sure of what I heard."

"No, tell me, Crystal! What did you hear?"

I watched as Crystal hesitated while she nervously began slicing the onion. But her hesitation only fed my curiosity. I needed to know what it was that she knew!

"Crystal, please! You know if the tables were turned, you'd want me to tell you. Or wouldn't you?"

"Okay, fine! Don't quote me on this but, earlier in the day, right before first period, I saw Melanie and Ms. Bloom talking in the classroom. And from what I heard...I don't know. It's silly!"

"Crystal, tell me!"

After she took a deep breath and put down the knife, Crystal looked me in the eye and said,

"Apparently, Ms. Bloom is a bit of a freak, if you know what I mean."

"No, I don't know what you mean!"

At that point, I was starting to see red! Crystal then took one last deep breath before saying,

"It would appear that... Melanie found a pair of Ms. Bloom's lingerie hanging inside her locker. She was pretty upset about it, and I think that's what they were arguing about this morning."

"What! That doesn't make any sense. Why would Ms. Bloom leave her underwear... Oh my goodness, are you telling me that they? No, no, it can't be. Melanie would never, she wouldn't!"

"You see, Gabrielle? That's why I didn't t want to say anything. I could have misheard. I could barely hear them, any-way!"

"No, Crystal. I think you heard perfectly well."

I don't think I have to tell you how upset I was. I was livid! But because I was a guest in Ms. Bailey's home, I wasn't going to run out with a bucket full of tears. If Ms. Bloom wanted to test me, fine. I was determined to show her who the child was and who was the adult in this situation. So I contin-ued helping out in the kitchen by cleaning and cooking the greens with Ms. Bailey's assistance, and I had nothing short of a smile on my face while doing so. But inside, I was dying for the opportunity to release a well-awaited storm of fury and rage, making sure that Melanie could feel every ounce of my pain.

After a couple of hours passed, and dinner was finally ready, everyone gathered around the dining room table. Ms. Bailey sat at the end of the table with her back facing the liv-ing room. Jesuse sat next to Ms. Bailey's right, and Josh was to her left. Then Crystal, of course, sat next to Josh, and Melanie took a seat next to Jesuse. I could tell that Melanie was ex-pecting me to sit next to her, but instead, I walked past her and took the open seat next to Crystal, which was diagonal from Melanie. It was fun, giving Melanie the cold shoulder for once, making her wonder, why me? Shortly after, every-one passed the food around until we all had some of every-thing on our plates. I couldn't deny that the smell of perfectly seasoned pork chops and greens did make my insides tingle, but only for a brief moment. Of course, as soon as I looked back up at Melanie, I was fuming again.

I COULDN'T understand why Gabrielle was all of a sudden giving me the stink eye. Her whole energy shifted. Anytime I made eye contact, smiled, or even breathed, it seemed like Gabrielle would do something to let me know how irritated she was. Even the way she was eating was angry. It was as if she was swallowing without tasting. I didn't know if something was said while I was stuck helping organize the garage, but I was eager to find out. And while I was in the garage packing, I was forced to listen to Josh and Jesuse ramble on for two hours about their favorite football teams, and when they moved on to wrestling, I was ready to scratch out my eyeballs. I mean, it's just mindboggling to me how guys can one day be at war with each other and then the next day be sitting in each other's lap. But, I didn't put much thought into it because I was too busy dodging fireball stares from Gabrielle. And not just that, but the whole drama club dinner was weird. Everyone, except for Josh and occasionally Crystal, was quiet. Then after Ms. Bailey had enough of the awkward silence, she looked up from her plate, smiled, and said,

"Why is everyone so quiet? Is the food that bad?"

"Oh no, not at all, Ms. Bailey! These pork chops are delish!" Josh interrupted with a mouth full.

"Well, I'm glad you like them!"

Then after that, one by one, everyone politely began complimenting Ms. Bailey on the food, which really was delicious, by the way. But after the compliments were all handed out, Ms. Bailey continued to stare in such a peculiar way and said,

"You know, you kids amaze me! And not in a funny laugh-out-loud sort of way, but in a way that amazes me to see that you all don't get how connected you really are. You guys are family! Maybe not by immediate blood or familiarity, but you are family. And yet, you treat each other like strangers. You allow your insignificant differences to keep you divided. When instead, you should welcome them and learn from them. And maybe you're right, Melanie, I guess I was trying to force you all into the same room so you guys could see what I see."

"And what do you see, Ms. Bailey?" Gabrielle asked with concern.

"That being at war with one another is pointless when you have yet to win the battle within yourselves. I didn't become a teacher because I wanted to teach textbooks or show how to light a stage correctly. I became a teacher because I wanted to inspire my students to grow intellectually and mentally. Textbooks won't prepare you for the world out there. Textbooks won't teach you how to navigate through everyday struggles. But learning true values, learning yourself, and building a good strong character, well that will prepare you for battles within."

"Ms. Bailey, I hate to interrupt because I do appreciate everything you've done for us. And the food was perfect! But are you okay? I mean, why are you telling us this, now?" Josh asked.

"Because I know that you all are graduating soon. You'll be off spreading your wings with the tiny bit of wisdom that you have. I just want to make sure that while you're out there flying through the world, that you fly with kindness. And also, remember that no matter what you decide to do in life, no matter what career path you choose, make sure that you become a part of something inspirational. Because if you're not spreading your wisdom, how will you make a difference? The kids coming up behind you and even yourselves, you guys will be the course."

I don't think that any of us knew what to say or even what to think. It was one of those teachable moments that you almost take for granted until life knocks you down, giving you a reason to look back and remember. A couple of us, I think, took heed sooner than others. It usually isn't until something significant happens that people take a moment to pause and examine their lives. I hoped that it wouldn't be the case with me as I looked up and listened. Then out of the blue, Crystal asked,

"Can I ask, Ms. Bailey, how come you never had children of your own? I mean, if my mother were more like you, I probably wouldn't have as many issues."

"Crystal, that was rude. Maybe she didn't want kids!" Josh blurted out.

"How was that rude? I was complimenting her!"

"Okay, hush now! It's okay. I guess life had different plans for me. And being older and wiser now, I wouldn't change a thing about my life even if I could. Although I would have liked to have gotten married, I never found anyone who could quite understand me. And that's okay! I realized years ago that some people were meant to have and teach children, while others were born to teach the world! Now enough of that, the food's getting cold."

"But wait, Ms. B, all that stuff in the garage, I thought

it belonged to your husband or something. But if you never married, then who does it belong to?" Jesuse asked.

"Oh, it belongs to my parents! Yeah, they decided to downsize from a five-bedroom house to a small two-bedroom apartment. My mom and dad had so much stuff, but I didn't want them getting rid of any of it. So, they gave me most of what they could, old clothes, pictures, and the pool table. I don't know; I just wanted something to have of theirs so that whenever they pass on, I could still feel connected to them, in a sense. You know?"

"Yeah, but I'm still confused. I mean, if you wanted to keep your parent's things as mementos, then why are you getting rid of them now?" Jesuse asked with concern.

"Boy, you guys ask a lot of questions! Come on and eat before the food gets cold!"

After Ms. Bailey awkwardly chuckled to herself and continued eating, neither of us knew what to say. It felt like she was withholding information or like she was urgently trying to prepare us for something. We got through the rest of the dinner with small talk and a few laughs. It strangely felt like we were starting to bond, thanks to Ms. Bailey. And when dinner was finally over, after Crystal and Josh had long left, Gabrielle and I were helping clean up in the kitchen. I could tell that something was on her mind, especially when she pulled me to the side and demanded that we talk. So, we excused ourselves, leaving Jesuse to finish helping wash the dishes. Once Gabrielle and I were outside, I walked us closer towards the driveway so that eavesdropping ears wouldn't be able to hear. The streetlight shined on both of us, and Gabrielle looked at me with those sad beautiful eyes and said,

"I've been trying my best all evening not to cause a scene, not to scream! But I cannot keep quiet any longer. I just need you to tell me the truth. And please, don't lie to me because that will just make things worse. I just need to know, are you having sex with her?"

"What are you... Who are you talking about?"

I was nervous! And I felt terrible that my gut reaction was to lie.

"Don't lie to me! I promise if you lie to me, and I find out the truth later, I will never forgive you! But, at least if you can be honest with me now, there might be some chance in the far, far-out future that I can forgive you. But please, tell me, are you?"

"NO! I'm not!"

"Have you ever?"

"Gabrielle, please...stop!"

"Stop what! Just tell me!"

"Gabrielle, I love you, okay? I love you, and..."

"You're really going to piss me off in a minute! Do you want to hear me scream, because I will? I will scream so loud that every person on this block will hear me! I mean, God, Melanie! I no longer have a relationship with my dad because of you. I came out for you! Did you have sex with her that night? Is that when it started?"

I couldn't lie anymore. I couldn't say a word. All I could do was stand there with my face wrinkled up in sadness, stalling for more time. But my time was up the moment I withheld the truth. The heartbreak on Gabrielle's face was so overpowering that I could feel her heart crumbling through my chest.

"Wow! So, this whole time...I was stupid! She's the reason you would barely touch me! And why were you with me? For charity?"

"No, of course not! Gabrielle, I..."

"Don't! Don't you dare speak! I sacrificed so much just to be with you because I loved you. Shame on me, though, for falling for a selfish, superficial brat who uses her childhood as a crutch to excuse her ignorant behavior. You're not the only person with a sad childhood. And you know what, I do hope she was worth every minute of pleasure because you just lost forever with me!"

"Gabrielle, wait, please!"

"Don't worry. I'm not going to turn your girlfriend into the police."

As Gabrielle stormed down the driveway to the sidewalk, I called out to her, begging her not to leave. But the more I followed, the more agitated she became. Finally, I had to back away and give her space to fume. I stopped at the end of the block and just stood there, watching as Gabrielle continued to storm out of sight. And while my feet became frozen in place, I was stuck, paralyzed in thought. Then after spending five minutes in a daze, I realized that it was time for me to do the one thing I should have done months ago. So, I picked up my feet and headed towards Ms. Bloom's house.

It was late in the evening, 6:40 P.M. to be exact when I got on the bus. I rode for nearly an hour before I reached my destination. I was eager to set things right. I didn't give any warning. I just showed up on Ms. Bloom's doorstep, hoping she would answer my knock. But after knocking and ring-ing the doorbell a few times, I was surprised that I didn't get an answer. Especially after seeing that her car was parked in the driveway. Something told me just to twist the doorknob, and so I did. How shocked I was to find out that she had left her front door unlocked. After walking inside, I noticed Ms. Bloom still had the lights on in the hallway and living room. I could also hear the sound of running water coming from upstairs. So, I got curious and slowly made my way up the staircase while shouting out her name. But there was still no response. As I made my way to the top of the stairs, closer to the bathroom, I could hear the shower water pouring out onto the bathtub floor and lightly brushing against the shower curtain.

I then tippy-toed my way inside, tapped on the shower curtain, and made my presence known; *Oh, Jesus Christ Melanie, you scared me*, she shouted. I apologized with my puffy eyes swollen from the large amounts of crying I did on the bus ride there. Ms. Bloom then rushed to turn off the water and asked that I hand her one of the towels that hung on the wall next to me, so I did. And as I stood in the bathroom, waiting for her to dry off, she began walking towards me with her left breast uncovered, crying out for me to touch. I quickly snapped out of it and asked,

"Can you cover yourself, please? We need to talk!"

Ms. Bloom then slowly wrapped herself up in the towel while standing inches away and asked,

"Is everything okay?"

"No, it's not…everything is a mess."

"Okay, well, give me a minute to get dressed, and we'll

talk. Do you want to wait for me in the kitchen? You should get yourself something to drink. You look parched."

"No, I'm fine... but if you want me to wait for you in the kitchen, I'll wait there."

"Well, I'd much rather you wait for me in the bed, but..."

"I'll be in the kitchen."

I had to shut that down quick! As tempting as she was, and I hated myself for even being swayed by her, it just proved even more how dangerous it was for me to be around her. I started to believe that part of me was addicted, that I needed her. But if needing her was going to cost me, Gabrielle, then I'd rather not need her at all. So, as I started to make my way back downstairs, I noticed a brown suit, jacket, and pants neatly hanging over a chair in her office. Curiosity got the best of me because, for one, I've never seen Ms. Bloom wear a pants suit, ever! And two, I couldn't tell if the clothes belonged to a woman or a man, but I had to find out!

As I walked inside, I quickly peeked around the room, then took a closer glance at the brown suit in front of me. I rubbed the material between my fingers, even bent down to get a whiff, but it oddly didn't smell like anything. So, I continued to examine the suit with my eyes while also keeping an ear out for the door. I was stumped. I couldn't figure out who the jacket and pants belonged to. I continued snooping around until I noticed a giant statue hanging on the wall right across from the desk. It was a beautiful African elephant painted in black with gold horns. Curiosity drew me to this object. I had never been inside Ms. Bloom's office because she always kept the door locked. But as I walked over and placed my hand on the elephant's trunk, a mechanism popped open below it, revealing a small drawer, and inside that drawer was a black cloth.

Whoa! Now that's when my heart really started to pound! I couldn't stop myself from snooping; I had to see what was inside. As I lifted the black cloth, underneath it revealed a shiny object, one I never thought I'd find in her house. Then, without thinking, I picked up that shiny object and slowly stepped away in disbelief. In my hands was a silver 9 mm magnum! What...The...Fuck! As I stood there staring down the barrel of the gun, I became startled when out of nowhere, I heard Ms. Bloom say five words that sent chills straight down my spine,

"He was aiming for you!"

"What!"

I turned around completely dumbfounded by her reply and watched as she continued to say,

"James...he was aiming for you, Melanie. I had no choice!

"You mean to tell me this whole time it was you? Why?"

I stood there shaking my head while holding the gun up to my chest. Ms. Bloom slowly walked toward me in her tan silk pajamas in an attempt to calm me down.

"Melanie, give me the gun, and I'll explain everything."

"Are there even any bullets left in this thing?"

"Just, give it to me, please! I don't want you to hurt yourself."

Ms. Bloom stood inches away while extending out her right hand, waiting for me to hand over the gun. I became hysterical, and I asked,

"You killed, James?"

"Melanie, give me the gun, now!"

I watched as she slowly grabbed the base of the gun out of my hands and walked towards the desk. Ms. Bloom then carefully placed the gun on the surface of the desk, next to the suit, and I continued to stare, not knowing what to think. Ms. Bloom then calmly walked back towards me as she tried to explain.

"I know you're probably confused right now. But I promise you, everything I did was to protect you."

"Protect me?"

"James had every intention of killing you! Okay, that's his gun! I couldn't just stand by and watch him take you away from me. I had to stop him, by whatever means necessary, to save you. And I'd make that same choice over and over again, for you!"

"I don't believe you. It doesn't make any sense. Why would James want to kill me? And what were you doing out there in the first place?"

"What do you think, Melanie? After seeing you and Gabrielle run out of the gym, my imagination got the best of me. But I'm glad I followed you. Otherwise, your body would be the one in a casket right now!"

I still didn't get it; I was puzzled!

"We need to go to the police! You need to turn yourself in. That family is suffering! You're the only person who can make it right."

"I can't do that, Melanie! You know I can't!"

"You mean you won't? Because you can do anything that you put your mind to if you try hard enough. Where's your conscience?"

"Melanie, if I turn myself in, I will spend the rest of my life in prison! You and I will never be able to be together. Is that what you want?"

"Is that the only thing you care about? You and I were never supposed to be together! I only came here to tell you that myself. I can't do this anymore."

"You can't…or you won't? Because you can do anything that you put your mind to, Melanie, remember? I was protecting you! And if that school had better security, if our government had stricter gun laws, we wouldn't be in this mess! So what was I supposed to do, huh, let him shoot you?"

"I'm done, I can't…I won't be a part of this anymore. And if I were you, I'd turn myself in while I still had the chance."

"What's that supposed to mean, Melanie? What does that mean?"

I stormed out of the room and back down the stairs while Ms. Bloom pleaded for me to stay, to stop, to listen! But I couldn't, I didn't. It was over. I think she knew it was over as well because the farthest she went after me was the front door. As I made my way outside and towards the sidewalk, I heard the sound of weeping fading away in the distance. My life had suddenly felt like a *John Singleton* film or a bad case of REM sleep. The sad part of it all was that the worst was still yet to come.

The next day, I debated with myself whether or not I should go to school. My heart wanted me to soak in bed all day, but my gut forced me out of bed and led me back down the halls of Lee Wallace High. And the halls were quiet, I thought, *odd*. I felt an uncomfortable chill running down my spine. I thought that it was the nerves from both of my breakups. My heart went from having more love than it could bear to feeling empty and cold. On my way to my locker, I didn't see Toni, Renee, Gabrielle, or Ms. Bloom in sight, not even Crystal or Josh. I took a deep breath as I went to use my combination and slowly opened my locker. While opening, I was reminded of the inappropriate surprise I found dangling in my face just twenty-four hours prior. But this time, I was stumped to find something more sinister hanging on the top shelf. I don't even think I had time to catch my breath before it happened.

The echoes coming from down the hall narrowed into a tiny buzzing in my ears. I felt my heartbeat flutter as though I were going to have a heart attack. I stood frozen in place for another minute until I finally heard distant shouting coming from down the hall. I looked toward my right, nothing. I then looked toward my left, and before I could even blink, I saw my entire life flashing before my eyes. Heading towards me were three police officers and two German shepherds. I don't think I need to tell you at this point what was sitting inside my locker staring at me dead in the eyes? It took me all of two seconds to realize what was about to happen. Suddenly, students were lining up in front of their lockers while the officers conducted their search.

By the time they reached my locker, the police officer had asked me to,

"Step aside, please!"

I broke down. I begged and pleaded, much like how Ms. Bloom did when I walked out on her. I guess it was senseless for me even to try and convince the officers that I was innocent, but I tried anyway.

"Please, just give me a chance to explain!"

"I'm only going to ask once more! Please, step aside!"

So, I did, slowly, and terrified out of my mind! I waited for the officer to reach inside my locker and find the metal object bestowed upon me by Ms. Bloom. That damn Ms. Bloom. All I could think was, how, why? The officers didn't ask me any questions because they didn't need to. They were sure they had the right person. I was minutes away from being another Black face sitting in a cage, trapped and powerless. Forget about logic and reasoning. When a person so badly wants the truth, they'll believe everything, including the lie, just to get it. That was the most humiliating moment of my life, being escorted down the hall in handcuffs while my peers, teachers, and faculty watched. Suddenly, everyone appeared, Josh, Crystal, Renee, Toni. Oh, and the look on Toni's face broke me the most. The way he glared at me with such conviction and then turned away in shame. It hurt me to the core, knowing he believed that I was capable of such a thing.

By the time Ms. Bailey stepped in line with the rest of the student body, I was too far gone down the hall. All I could hear was her shouting in the distance, demanding answers. And right when I was almost out the door, I saw Gabrielle and Ms. Bloom standing on opposite sides of the hallway directly in front of each other, watching as I walked away. Gabrielle could barely look at me, and Ms. Bloom had the nerve to turn away in shame. She didn't even try to stop what was happening; she just allowed me to walk out of the building, taking the heat for her committed crime. I remember thinking to myself as I took one last glance at Ms. Bloom that; *if this is the true definition of love, then love must be a powerful lie!*

| 10 |

SECRETS

WHAT THE *hell have I done?* That question was the only question I could ask myself, over and over again. They say love makes you do stupid things. Well, love made me act in high lunacy! I swear, I never meant for Melanie to take the fall. I only put the gun in her locker to scare her a little! I had no idea that Principal Settle was going to order another search. The first time the police searched the school was the day after, well, you already know it without me saying it. But I was left in the dark when the police showed up again, parading our halls. You can believe what you will; I honestly had no idea what was happening until it was too late! What could I do? Step forward and shout with my wrists extended; *you've got the wrong girl. It's me you want!* I let the one person who held the biggest piece of my heart be arrested for a crime that shouldn't have even made itself into existence in the first place.

I even began questioning my character, feeling like a terrible person for not standing up and doing the right thing. For the rest of the day, all I could do was replay the look on

Melanie's face as the police took her away. I wondered for a brief moment before Principal Settle rushed everyone back to their appropriate classes if I even deserved to step foot back into my classroom and teach again. Did I even have the right to beg Melanie for her forgiveness after displaying such cowardice? I knew I had to do something. But before I could, I needed to examine my life and the choices I made that led up to this hideous nightmare. The farthest I could go back was my earliest memories, my childhood.

It all began when I was in elementary school, third grade. I was the happiest little girl, at least I felt so! I was never without a smile on my face. I was also very attentive and got mostly A's, with a couple of B's here and there. Math was my least favorite subject, but I tried my best not to go below a C. Of all the grades, I remembered 3rd grade the most. It was a life changing year for me. I didn't have many friends; I mostly stayed to myself until I met Julie. She was the sweetest! Julie was a new student who transferred schools during the middle of the school year. It was December. I remember it well because there was lots of snow on the ground, and Mrs. Williams, my teacher at the time, was throwing a winter party for the class.

Some of the parents brought in different treats, while others brought samples of home-cooked meals. And my favorite, OHH, my absolute favorite, was this Asian-inspired dish. It was homemade vegetable stuffed egg rolls and noodles! Wonderful! But not to lose the point, Julie and I became close as we did everything together. I found myself becoming more and more attracted to her as time went on. I didn't fully understand my feelings at first; I just knew that I loved being around her. Julie made my tiny little heart flutter. And when I found out that the feeling was mutual, we acted on our impulses. Julie and I shared our first kiss outside on the playground. And mind you, back then in the '80s, being gay was very much taboo. So when a few of the teachers saw my sweet Julie and me kissing at the top of the slide during recess, all hell broke loose! The kids around us were pointing and laughing, saying; *eww, gross*! You know how children are.

We had no idea that our innocent kiss would lead to so much bigotry and fear. One of the teachers sent Julie and me to the principal's office, and we waited for our parents to pick us up from school. Suspension is what we got over a simple, innocent kiss. Ha! Imbeciles!

I remember sitting in the principal's office with my legs crossed, staring at the bottoms of my shinny white dress shoes, wishing that I wouldn't get in trouble. Though I quickly realized that wishful and naive thinking would get me nothing but disappointment in life. Prayer, on the other hand, I found would carry me through the next five years of my life. My mother was a fool in love, and a fool she was, may she rest in peace. I'd like to think that she lived a full life. She was 72 when old age took her away. But when my mother was alive, she was constantly on the prowl for love. I believe she had more men in her life than I had hair follicles. Okay, maybe that was a tad dramatic. But my mother was never alone.

So while I sat in the principal's office on the verge of tears, waiting for my mommy to come and get me, I was taken aback when I saw that her boyfriend of the month showed up instead. This man was rough around the edges, wore a shaggy beard, short Afro, and he always dressed in these pressed jeans and polo shirts. His name was Marques. Marques worked as an electrician, from what my mother told me. It just seemed like Marques spent most of his time with my mother and me than at work! So yes, I was surprised when HE walked into the principal's office expecting to pick me up. I didn't understand, and I didn't feel at all comfortable being alone with him. The car ride home was tortious. He kept asking me odd questions like; have I ever kissed a boy, did I like boys, those kinds of questions. And even as a child, I knew a little something about boundaries. Marques tried to be friendly by telling me how pretty I was, how I looked just like my mother. He even complimented me on my legs, which made me want to vomit!

And of course, while he sickeningly whispered those compliments, he was eyeing my chest and thighs the entire time. Talk about feeling like a piece of meat. I thought to tell Marques to keep his eyes on the road, but instead, I turned toward the window, wishing that he'd soon shut his trap! Eventually, he did as we parked in the driveway of my south side home on the cul de sac. I became frightened when I noticed that my mother's car wasn't parked outside. Then as Marques and I got out and walked up to the front door, I asked,

"Where's my mom?"

"Oh, your mom? She's not here; she's at work. That's why I picked you up, princess! But don't be sad. Now, you get to have some fun with your uncle Marky Mark."

Marky Mark? Oh, I couldn't stand it when he'd refer to himself in the third person. It was repulsive. He was repulsive! All I wanted to do was go to my room, lock the door, and challenge myself to a puzzle. Sadly, I didn't have a lock on my door, at least not one that worked. And when Marky Mark helped himself inside my room and sat on the corner of my bed, I looked at him like he was senseless! He just ogled me as I reached into my closet for a hanger to hang up my jacket. Afterward, I kept my good eye on his crooked smile and the other on my dresser while reaching for one of my puzzles. I then found a seat far away from the bed, on the floor, in the corner of my room. Marques just continued to stare and eventually asked,

"Why are you sitting on the floor? I won't bite, princess. Come on up here, sit next to me!"

Marques freakishly rubbed my comforter on top of my bed in a circular motion as he waited for me to get up. And while I ignored every bone in my body, every quiet voice telling me to run, I instead found myself sitting right next to him. I felt a sudden chill come over me, goosebumps. I just examined his body language, tried to ignore every word that flowed out of his mouth, every word until he asked,

"So, what's this about you kissing girls at school? Are they confusing over there? That's wrong, Jennifer! Girls aren't supposed to be kissing other girls! A girl is supposed to kiss a boy, like me. Do you see? And I got some nice juicy lips. You like my lips, princess?"

"No! I don't like boys!"

"Well, maybe that's because you never had a boy ask you out before. But you want to know a secret? If I was in your class, I'd ask you to be my girlfriend. You're so pretty, the way you smile, you're very special, you know that? And sitting next to you makes me feel special. Why don't you give me your hand; I'll show you just how special you make me feel."

Before I knew it, Marques was unfastening his pants, exposing his sizeable hideous eggplant in front of me. I knew something wasn't right with him the first day I met him. How on Earth my mother was oblivious to it was beyond me. But when Marques grabbed my hand and forced me to touch him, I wanted to cry. I was only EIGHT YEARS OLD, and Julie was the first and only person I had ever wanted to kiss. My mind wasn't ready for what was to come next with Marques. What I was doing, what he was doing, didn't feel right at all. And when Marques reached into my panties, I felt beyond violated. I felt like my body no longer belonged to me, like someone else; this stranger controlled my movements, decisions, ME! To cope, I had to think of a place far away from reality, where I felt safe.

Then after Marques went for lift-off, I was left alone in my room, crying to my dolls and stuffed teddy bears. Contrary to Marques's illogical belief, what he did to me only reaffirmed my interest in girls. Marques used my homosexuality as an excuse to justify his actions. And when he went from being man of the month to man of the year, he proposed to my mother, and they wed. Marques was my stepfather for the next decade. You'd think that a man would be satisfied with one woman, especially when she was putting out every five minutes, but no, he had a bigger appetite for little old me. When I turned ten years old, Marques found himself growing bored of his disgusting foreplay. And that's when he began forcing himself on top of me.

Growing up in a home like that, feeling like an only child because my two elder siblings were decades older than me, and flew halfway across the country to pursue their careers in Family Law and Medicine, was torture! And though I heavily prayed, I wasn't very religious. I didn't believe in a man-constructed God because I disagreed with all the God is Man, and Man is a woman's reason for being hogwash. I believed in a God that truly loved everyone. And I prayed to my God, every single day, every time Marques would lay himself on top of me, and every time he'd gaze in my direction, I prayed. By the time I was in high school and started to develop, Marques fell less attracted to me and lost interest. The human mind deeply astonishes me! And would you believe that when Marques drifted away from me, I felt jealous? I had gotten so used to being abused that I felt like something was wrong with me when it stopped. How insane is that?

I knew that I would need decades of therapy to undo what he did, but I'll save that for another time. Back to me being a freshman at Lee Wallace High, and yes, how ironic is it that I years later ended up becoming a teacher at the very same school I attended as a teenager? I had many plans for myself, goals I wanted to achieve, and countries I wanted to visit once I finished high school, but life had other plans for me. In my freshman year of high school, I didn't have many friends. I was just getting used to exploring my new freedom. It felt like the world was my oyster, and there were so many beautiful girls all around me. They all seemed so confident in themselves, and I wasn't. My confidence took years to come. I had a lot of brainwashing to undo and self-loving to learn.

So, one day, my sophomore year, I sat in the cafeteria with

a couple of the kids from the drama department. They were very engaging, but my mind was elsewhere. It wasn't until someone bold and fiesty sat down in front of me, catching my attention, that I snapped back into reality.

"Hey, Earth to Mars, anyone home?"

"Excuse me?" I asked.

"Sorry, you looked like you needed saving. Are you good?"

"Yes, I'm good! Actually, no! This school is quite boring. I think you and I are the only Black people in this entire building!"

"Well, you clearly haven't been around many Black people using words like; Quite! Tell me, do you read a lot of books? You must read a lot of books."

"Yes, but…wait, what's wrong with the way I speak? And how would you have said what I just said?"

"Girl, I would say; *it's fuckin boring in this bitch*! Just like that!"

"Fine… it's fuckin boring in this bitch!"

We laughed so hard that the kids sitting at the table next to us got up and moved away. She then asked,

"So, what's your name?"

"Jennifer…Jennifer Bloom, and you are?"

"I'm Monica…Monica Howard, but you can call me Mo." She mimicked.

Monica, Howard! How crazy is that? I found myself befriending the one person in the entire world who would soon be responsible for birthing my true happiness, Melanie. I had no idea what the future would bring as Monica and I grew thick as thieves. All through sophomore and junior year, we did almost everything together. We walked to school together, played hooky together, and we even studied together. Then halfway during junior year, our tiny little bubble widened. Monica began dating heavily, and by doing so, we met other people, Black people, in the community. It was vital that we didn't lose our sense of self while being seahorses in an ocean filled with jellyfish. Then after a while, I started to notice that Monica's relationships were becoming abusive. Each relationship she'd get into would last a semester.

But Monica and I's friendship was finally tested the summer right before senior year. Her family was throwing a pre-Fourth of July barbeque. I was invited along with her boyfriend at the time, Eric. Mind you, Monica lived out in the middle of nowhere Woods-Ville, and for me, that warranted providing my own transportation, just in case. Thankfully I was smart enough to save the money I made working part-time at the local grocery store. I was seventeen when I bought my first car, a 1985 two-door Toyota Corolla. So, back to the barbeque, it was around 4 P.M. when I arrived, and the smell of barbequed hot dogs, hamburgers, and steaks drew me in with a hungry belly and a bright smile. So many people gathered outside; I had never seen so many black people together like that before. It was pleasant until it wasn't. Once it was time to sit down and eat finally, Monica, Eric, and I grabbed one of the picnic tables closest to the backdoor patio. The boom box was playing *Earth Wind and Fire*, and everyone was having a good time grooving to the music. Suddenly our table of three grew to eight. I sat next to Monica, and Eric was to the left of her. Monica's parents sat across from us along with her grandfather. The two others at the table were Monica's cousins, and they filled the empty spaces as we all sat close together.

I didn't realize how Christian she and her family were until the awkward Godly conversations began. I couldn't even get through my first bite of food without being questioned about my relationship status or being complimented on my looks by one of Monica's cousins.

"So Jennifer, you got a boyfriend?"

"Isaiah, leave that girl alone. She doesn't want you!" Monica's dad interrupted.

"I was just asking a question! You know, making conversation."

Then Monica's mother interrupted with,

"She's too beautiful to be single! But even if you are honey, I'm sure that God has the right man in store for you! He may not come when you want him, but he's always on time!"

Then almost everyone at the table added an,

"AMEN!"

Oh, and then Monica's grandpa also had a few words to share from scripture.

"God is the Alpha and the Omega! God sees all, hears all, knows all, and speaks all through us! And as such, he created us as miniature gods to take care of our women. I think sometimes we forget that, especially with this new generation coming up. But Isaiah, don't listen to your auntie! If you want this pretty little thing to be your queen. Seek her out! Grab her and hold tight, and remember, you can do anything through Jesus Christ our Lord!"

Did this man just use Jesus to make his point? Uh, after

years of having one man trying to force heterosexuality into my vagina, it was an obvious trigger when another tried to force it down my ears. And before Isiah could position himself to dare ask me to be his princess, or whatever, I blurted out,

"I'm sorry, but I'm not sure that I belong here. I'm not who you all think that I am."

The awkward stares began to set in. Monica looked at me with confusion, and then her mother asked,

"What do you mean, honey? Of course, you belong here. You're one of us; you'll always be welcome into our family."

"With all due respect, ma'am, I live my life differently, according to freedom of choice. Not built on biblical rules. I just can't sit here pretending to be someone I'm not. I understand and respect that you all are very religious people, but that's not the kind of God I believe in."

"That's okay, sweetie…everyone finds Jesus in their own time. All you need is the right boy to guide you. He will lead your heart to the right place."

Right then is when I slammed my fists against the wooden table and shouted,

"I don't need a man, boyfriend, or anyone, to guide me anywhere! I am my own person; I'm strong, independent, a leader! But more importantly and to the point, I'm gay! I am super fucking gay, and I won't apologize or continue to be punished for it!"

Monica had no idea, or at least I didn't think that she did. I kept that part of myself secret, and for a good reason. I always felt in my gut that she would disapprove. I wanted her friendship so badly that I was willing to sacrifice who I was and my values just to have it. And at that moment, I saw Monica look at me with such disappointment, a look I'd never seen before. I knew it was time for me to go. But not before her family had last-minute questions.

"Monica, did you know this? Are you funny too?" Her mother asked.

"No, I had no idea," Monica replied.

Monica's father then looked at me and said,

"This may not be any of my business, but Jennifer, how do you know for sure that this is the lifestyle you want to live? I mean, have you ever even been with a boy before?"

"Two things, Mr. Howard; One, being gay isn't a lifestyle no more than being straight is. And two, I think I've had enough dick in me this lifetime to last a millennium!"

I left Monica's family sitting at the table more curious than children gathering around the chimney on Christmas eve. What hurt most was finding out how a difference in preference ended up costing me years of friendship. And I never told anyone about my rapist, not even my mother. I think it was partly due to me thinking she wouldn't believe me because she'd choose him, or I waited too long to mention it. And if my mother would have believed me, how would I explain all those years of silence? So I held onto the pain for 20 years before I finally sought out counseling.

Monica and I went from being the best of friends to not even acknowledging each other whenever we'd pass each other in the halls. It's crazy how little weight the word friendship or friend has to it. The slightest argument, disagreement, or difference could wipe away its entire existence. I never imagined that Monica and I would get to a place of pretending we didn't exist to each other. And as the years went by, after high school, I worked on myself, my self-healing, and I watched myself transform from that timid, naive little girl to a powerhouse! Little did I know that I still had years of self-work to do. I earned a master's degree in teaching. And with the help of grants and my savings, I bought a beautiful two-story home on the west side of town.

Monica, on the other hand, I heard, wasn't doing too great after high school. World on the streets was that Monica started getting herself in trouble with the law. It wasn't until one day, a few weeks after I graduated college, that I ran into Monica downtown in the fall of 96. It was a sunny afternoon when I made my way out of the post office and saw Monica walking in my direction. It was a total shock to see her after all those years. She looked so different, lifeless, and defeated. Monica tried to put on a show pretending she was ecstatic to see me, but I could read between the lines. Still, I was as cordial as I could be while I tried to keep up with the conversation. That was until Monica awkwardly disclosed to me that she was pregnant and was trying to have an abortion! She even had the nerve to ask me to go with her and pay because she needed my emotional and financial support.

I was so insulted and disgusted with her that I just walked away without saying another word. It would have been one thing if we had stayed friends, but I couldn't help feeling used. The way Monica treated me after I came out to her and her family, I don't think I have been able to forgive her to this day for that kind of heartbreak! But that day was the last time I saw Monica, until recently, since knowing Melanie. And before I met Melanie, I was much like my mother, going from person to person searching for true love. I never imagined I'd find myself falling for one of my students, let alone Monica's own daughter! The first time I saw Melanie, though, I knew right away who she was. Of course, I did, Melanie had her mother's smile, but it was a relief to know that she had Ms. Bailey's heart. And speaking of Ms. Bailey, Lynda, she and I became acquaintances on my first day teaching at Lee Wallace High in August of 2012. I remember her having so much wisdom and knowledge to share.

Lynda became like an older sister to me. Unlike the two sisters I had by blood, Ms. Bailey was always there when I needed advice or even just a laugh. Our friendship didn't go beyond the walls of Lee Wallace High until 2015, when Lynda invited me to Melanie's 17th birthday party. As I stated before, it was never my intention to fall in love with one of my students. I would purposely date women older than me so that I wouldn't fall into the spectrum or classified list of the stereotypical abused. They say hurt people hurt people; Well, I can confidently say that there was nothing but love in my heart when it came to Melanie. And how can we judge one another, as if sins come with a grading point scale? Please, let's not assume that one person's sin holds less weight than the other. I don't compare my relationship, my love for Melanie, to the horrors I've been through as a child. Even I had to forgive my rapist or begin the process because I refused to hold him accountable for my pain. To forgive sickness, I learned that one must be willing to try and understand it.

And though I'm still working through the forgiving process, I found that I at least could begin to understand the imperfections of the human race. Maybe it's easier to understand sickness once you're standing on the other side of it wearing the gown. But there was nothing sick about my feelings for Melanie. They were and still are, true! Now I'll take you back to the night of the dance where it all began; Yes! Curiosity bit me hard in the ass, and as a result, I found myself following Melanie and Gabrielle out of the gymnasium and behind the school. It was extremely dark, but I could see the two of them talking from where I was standing. I heard footsteps following behind me, and I got nervous, so I moved further inward, where I saw Toni talking to James. I lost sight of Melanie because some *idiot* was trying to scare me. Anyway, after another three to four minutes of eavesdropping, I heard the same noise, foot tracks moving towards me again.

I was becoming agitated at this point as I tried to get away without being seen. Instead, I was scared deeper into the woods where James and Toni were standing. I could hear them clearly, and the next thing I knew, Toni was stormy away, leaving James standing alone, conflicted and irate. I immediately had the thought to sneak my way back inside because I had begun to feel like a silly child, especially after hearing Josh, Crystal, and Jesuse arguing in the distance. So, I waited for James to start walking when I followed behind. While I was sneaking my way out of the woods behind James, I noticed that he reached into his back pocket for something. I didn't think anything of it at first, not until he revealed a silver gun, one that brightly stood out in the dark. I didn't have time to think about what he was going to do. My only thought was to stop him and protect Toni. But when I stood up and saw that James was pointing the gun at Melanie in the near distance, I rushed up behind and whispered for him to put down the gun.

I was successful at first as I startled him into shock mode. Then when James re-pointed the gun at me, I was triggered, and defense mode kicked into high gear when I used all my strength to wrestle the gun out of his hands and into mine. After struggling, I thought to knee James in the groin, which caused him to become unsteady, allowing me to slip free to the ground, landing on my back, with the gun in my hands. Then without thinking, still in fight mode, just as James was ready to pounce, I pulled the trigger. It took everything inside of me to hold back my tears because I knew a child had just died by my hand. The bullet pierced right through his left skull, and suddenly, it was silent outside. And while everyone was becoming distracted by the sound of gunfire, I was quietly whimpering my way to the side entrance of the school woods when out of nowhere, I heard a familiar voice whisper,

"Well, well, well... Now Ms. Bloom, I never pegged you to be a killer! Bravo!"

The sick boy just stood there silently clapping his hands with a grin forcing me to ask,

"Biscuit...Timothy! What are you doing out here?"

"Oh please, don't call me that! You know how I feel about my government name; only my mom still calls me Timothy. And as far as what I'm doing, well, looks like I'm about to help the police solve a murder."

"Are you insane?" I snarled.

"You know what, Ms. Bloom, now that you mention it, I think I might be!"

"Try as you might to intimidate me, but it's not going to work! If I have to go down, I promise I will drag your ass down right along with me! With your history and even the goddamn present, you've created so many messes that even a janitor couldn't keep up with you. You're a clown! A sick, demented clown who needs an old-fashioned ass whooping! Who do you think they'll believe anyway? A teacher who graduated top of her class, loved by most of her students? Or a child who throws temper tantrums because he's insecure and afraid of change?"

As Biscuit and I hid behind one of the trees out of sight, a rush of teachers and students began heading our way. That was until Principal Settle ordered everyone to stay back. I then pulled the gun out from the back of my skirt and dared the boy to turn me in.

"Here, go on, take it! You'll need proof. Maybe by turning me in, you'll finally be able to sleep better at night, that is until you're sleeping on a cot in the prison next door to mine. So here, Timothy, what are you waiting for?"

I tried to hold my gaze and show no weakness as I heard Principal Settle making her way closer, shining her flashlight in our direction. My heart began to race, but I kept my hold, waiting for Biscuit to make his move.

"Nah, I think watching you squirm in your chair will be worth the wait. Eventually, the police will figure out the truth, and the longer it takes them, the more satisfying it'll be to watch when they catch you!"

Biscuit backed down and turned away as he blended into

the crowd. While everyone was becoming distracted by James, I was sneaking my way back inside. I quickly made my way to the security room because I knew that one of the first pieces of evidence the police would ask for would be the security footage. So I had to hurry, review the camera footage and delete it so it wouldn't show me walking into the hallway and out of the building. It also helped that I learned a thing or two about surveillance systems during my college days. I even knew where most of the blind spots were at the school to avoid drawing attention to myself when I snuck out of the gymnasium. I guess being a teacher did come with its own set of perks. But none of that mattered.

The truth was that I was the kind of person who, in the end, couldn't even protect and save the person I claimed to love most in the world. I was selfish! I am selfish. After watching the officers escort Melanie out of the school like some criminal, I spent the rest of the day hiding from my feelings just so I could make it through. And by the time the day was over, I was ready to drive down to the county jail and make things right. That was until an unwanted presence standing in the doorway interrupted me by saying,

"It's a shame that after all these months, they ended up catching the wrong person. Are you really going to let her take the fall for you?" Biscuit asked.

He just smugly stood there, expecting me to beg for his continued silence.

"I don't know what you're talking about, Timothy. But school is out for the day. So why don't you hurry on home like a good little boy, hmm?"

"Damn! And I thought I was heartless. Well, it doesn't

matter much to me anyway. At least they'll be putting one of you in a cage."

"Get out! And go find a hobby or something to do besides pestering the hell out me!"

There was something truly demented about that boy. And I wasn't in any kind of mood to psychoanalyze him. As I started to walk closer towards the doorway where Biscuit, Timothy, whatever his name, was still standing, I was caught off guard again by Ms. Bailey as she came rushing inside past the two of us and said,

"Oh, I'm so glad I found you before you left. I need your help…

"Just a moment Lynda. Is there anything else I can help you with, Timothy?"

"Nope! All good here, Ms. Bloom."

I waited for the menace to walk out of the doorway and turn the corner before giving Ms. Bailey my full attention. Before I could speak a word, she nervously added,

"We need to get Melanie out of there, now! She didn't do this, Jennifer; she couldn't even kill the spiders on her wall! Melanie wouldn't hurt anyone! Right?"

"No, of course not. I was actually on my way to the jail to see if there was anything that I could do."

"Good! We have to do something! You know how they treat our people. They will be quick to convict her without question. You see how quickly they just took her out of here?"

"Lynda, please, take a breath. Everything will be okay. We just need to…"

And then it happened, she showed up and stormed her

way into my classroom looking a hot mess, I might add, startling Ms. Bailey and myself as she shouted,

"What the hell is going on! What did you two do to my daughter?"

"Hold on a minute! How did you get past security? AGAIN?" I sternly asked.

"Oh, please! I spent over half a decade in federal prison. I learned how to sneak my way around a guard or two. Now back to my question, what the hell did you two buffoons get my daughter into?"

"You're daughter? You're hilarious; you know that? You haven't given a damn about Melanie since she was a fetus. So don't march in here pretending as if you care. I will call security if I have to!"

"Call security? Bitch, have you forgotten that I know who you are and what you've been doing with my daughter? If anyone is going to call security, it should be me!"

"Enough! I can't take anymore!" Ms. Bailey shouted.

After getting our attention, Monica and I noticed Ms. Bailey struggling as she walked over toward my desk and slowly sat down in the chair. I glared with concern as I followed and sat on the edge of my desk and asked,

"Are you okay?"

"I'm fine… I just have a hard time breathing sometimes, and I get dizzy. It comes and goes!" Ms. Bailey replied.

"Well, you don't look or sound fine at all. Lynda, please, it's me. Just tell me, what's going on?"

While waiting anxiously for Ms. Bailey to say something

other than *I'm fine*, Monica rudely let out a loud sigh as she hovered nearby.

"I'm sick…I was recently diagnosed with heart disease. I've been having issues with my heart, my breathing for a while now. It was easier to cover up and hide until a few days ago. But the way you two are acting, the way that you talk to each other, you're about to drive me into having a heart attack!"

"But heart disease, Lynda?" I replied.

"I don't care about what's going on between the two of you, but Melanie, she needs us. I don't want her believing that I don't care about her."

"No, Lynda, Melanie knows how much you care. Have you told her; does she know?"

"No, she doesn't! You're the first."

I felt terrible while sitting on the edge of my desk, trying to comfort Lynda as I rubbed her shoulder. I didn't want to add to her stress, but someone else in the room rudely didn't give a damn.

"Hey, I'm sorry that you're dying of heart problems, Ms. Bailey. And I do appreciate everything that you've done for my daughter up until this point. But, you both need to get Melanie out of jail before the court convicts and sends her to prison. Melanie will not survive a day in prison, trust me! So, if you two want to hold hands and sing kumbaya, do it on your own time! But this time belongs to Melanie," Monica replied.

I had enough of Monica's blatant disrespect. I was ready to give her a piece of my mind, but by the time I opened my mouth, Monica was on her way out the door. I waited with Ms. Bailey until she was well enough to stand, and then I drove us downtown to the jail. With Ms. Bailey's state of mind, her condition, I didn't trust her getting behind the wheel. The entire ride there, I felt nothing but guilt and her unspoken distrust. It felt like Ms. Bailey wanted to ask me something but was afraid to vocalize it. Or again, it could have just been my guilt. When we finally arrived at the jail, the police did everything they could to keep us in the dark. We couldn't even speak to Melanie; they gave us this whole rundown about needing to be added to the visitation and call list. They were so aggressive with us that I had to keep Ms. Bailey and me from making a scene. And as a result, we left there that evening with less information than we walked inside with. I knew that I was the only person holding the key to Melanie's freedom, but I was desperate to find a way to where we both could both be free.

Sadly, instead of freeing Melanie, I let months pass by without saying a damn thing. I felt ashamed, like I couldn't face her until I had a solution to save both of us. I, however, was running out of time. After being added to Melanie's visitation list and summoning up the courage, I decided to see her. It was right before graduation. I had it all rehearsed in my mind knowing what I would say. Then right when I took a seat and stared at Melanie through the thick glass that separated us, I was speechless for the first time. Holding back the tears that were making their way to the corners of my eyes, I watched as Melanie glared at me with animosity, and I prepared myself for what she had to say.

"So, are you going to say something? Or are you just going to sit there and stare at me the entire time?"

"I-I'm sorry, I don't know what to say. I just knew that I had to see you."

"It's been three months...THREE! And you don't know what to say? How about, I'm sorry, Melanie, for being so selfish, for thinking only of myself and my needs? Why don't you start there?"

"You don't understand, Melanie! I have been doing everything that I can to try and get you out of here! This was never supposed to happen; you were never supposed to end up in here."

"Really? Well, why don't you tell that to the person who planted a murder weapon in my locker?"

"Melanie... I was just as shocked as you were."

"How? How is that even possible when you're on the damn payroll?"

"Melanie, please... I need you to know how much I do care about you. Lee Wallace hasn't been the same without you. Your teachers, your friends, ME...we haven't been the same..."

"Changing the subject, I see... Look, why don't you cut the dramatics and save it for someone who's got the money to buy tickets to your show and get me the hell out of here!"

"I'm doing everything I can!"

"Sitting behind a desk saying better her than me isn't doing shit to get me out of here!"

I froze. I knew that Melanie was right. The guilt of it all was killing me. Yet, I just continued to stare with a bent face and watery eyes.

"So when were you going to tell me?" Melanie asked.

"Tell you what?"

"All these years, and you never said a word. But now, it's all starting to make sense."

"What are you talking about, Melanie?"

"You...and my mother! You knew her before she made the newspapers. You both graduated from Lee Wallace High, my high school! I always just assumed that you went to school somewhere else, a different city, even. I didn't think to connect the dots..."

"Melanie..."

"There's no point in lying. I'm most likely going to die in here anyway, or prison. But tell me, is that why you took such an odd interest in me? Have you secretly been in love with my mother this whole time?"

"What? NO! I swear Melanie, I don't know what that woman has told you, but your mother and I were just friends and for a very brief moment in time!"

"Then why couldn't you tell me that? Why didn't you? You know what...forget it! I realize that all I've been to you is a pawn on your chessboard. My entire life has been nothing but an over-extended matinee filled with masked characters. And you know the worse part about this epiphany? It's realizing that it was never written for me to be loved. I think that maybe I really am just...unlovable."

"Melanie, don't say that. You know that's not true! Dammit, I love you!"

"Yeah, I can tell! Uhm, I don't... I don't want to see you anymore. I don't want to hear your voice; I'm done. It's time for this play to end, for the curtains to close for good. I hope that you'll do the right thing but, I'm not holding my breath!"

Melanie then stood up, and I pleaded with her not to go.

"Wait, Melanie, please, just give me a little bit more time!"

"Our time is up, in here, and out there. Goodbye, Jennifer."

We exchanged one last look before the guard took her away. I felt my heart rip into two as I watched Melanie walk back out of my life. What hurt me the most was knowing I would let her spend another night in that horrible place because I was more concerned for my life rather than thinking of the harm I was doing to hers. I truly believed the judge would go easier on Melanie due to her age. And if she could say that it was all in the name of self-defense, then I believed it would help her case even more. How did I sleep at night, you might wonder? I didn't! I'd lie awake wondering if I'd ever find the courage to do the right thing. Or I'd wonder if I would continue to hide away from the truth, hoping that hour by hour, the guilt I carried would lesson. Because at the end of the day, I sadly did believe it was better her…than me.

| 11 |

GRADUATION

IT WAS officially May 25th, 2017, graduation day! It has been one long, exhausting, heartbreaking year, and although our high school days were coming to an end, the real trouble was only just beginning. At our school, they made us rehearse the graduation walk; did you have to do that? Did you like it? Because I thought it was a waste of fucking time. The entire student body got to watch while we marched the halls and gymnasium like God's, as they waited to take our place as the new, *Senior Class*. I didn't think I'd make it this far with everything that happened. Thank God, though, that I had Ms. B around to help me get my life back on track. Ever since Melanie pled guilty, things have taken a dramatic turn for the worse. I watched while, week after week, Ms. Bailey's health started to decline. At first, I thought it was just old age, the flu, or again, old age.

But when Ms. Bailey woke up with chest pains and sweats one night, I knew that it was severe. It was heartbreaking to see; it reminded me of my mother all over again. I guess, in a way, Ms. B became like a Godmother to me. I learned so much from her in those five months of living with her. She taught me patience, she taught me forgiveness, but more importantly, she taught me love. And with each of those lessons she instilled in me, I made sure to repay that love tenfold. People always say that things happen for a reason. Well, I believe I was placed there for Ms. Bailey right when she needed someone the most. Neither of us had ever thought that it would be Melanie sitting in a jail cell. And it didn't add up to any of us. I think the stress of it all is what caused Ms. Bailey's condition to worsen quicker.

She was so consumed with Melanie's case, trying to find the person she believed to be responsible, that she neglected herself in the process. I did any and everything I could to make sure that Ms. Bailey was eating, resting, even doing breathing exercises when needed, but it was a challenge. You know Ms. B; stubborn as a mule and doesn't stop until she gets what she wants. I'm glad, however, that Ms. Bailey didn't give up on me. I understood why Melanie praised her so and didn't want me encroaching on her space. And speaking of stubborn mules, I decided to visit Melanie a week before graduation to catch her up to speed and see how she was doing. Of course, Melanie was thoroughly displeased to see me. I just smiled as I sat on the side of freedom and hoped she give me at least five minutes to speak.

"So, have you come here to gloat or what?" Melanie asked.

"Gloat? No, of course not. I just wanted to see how you've been holding up! And also, I didn't know if there were any butch lesbians in here that I needed to scare off for you."

"Uhm, I'm a butch lesbian...sort of, so no. And you don't have to come in here putting on some little brother act to try and make me think that you care. Just tell me what you want so I can get back to my nap."

"I do care, Melanie. And I know that we haven't been the best of friends, but why do we have to be enemies? I mean, I get that I've been ignorant about the whole gay thing in the past, but this year has taught me a lot. Ms. Bailey helped me see things differently and see people in a light that I had no idea existed. Since losing my mom, I felt like I had to fill her shoes sooner than I was ready to, but I'm doing it! I'm taking the lessons she taught me, and I'm taking my life into my own hands! I'm even considering going to college, something I never thought I'd do."

"Ah! So, you are here to gloat."

"No, no, I'm sorry, I'm just trying to make a point."

"Do you know that I have court two days before graduation? Two days…and then the judge will decide whether or not to throw me in prison for the rest of my life or sentence me to death row."

"Wait, no, they can't do that! They can't try you as an adult."

"They can do it, and they are doing it! I've been sitting in here for three months waiting for a guard to walk by my cell, call my name, and release me from this menstrual-filled nightmare. But every day that passes, and I'm still sitting in here staring at these bars, my hope bar decreases more and more. My lawyer even told me that because I was eighteen when James was murdered, and he was seventeen, they can try me as an adult. They don't care about reasoning or finding the missing pieces to make this case make fucking sense; me being black was the only piece they needed to make it stick.

"And Jesuse… I've always heard of these things happening to people on the news or some movie on the lifetime channel, but never in a million years did I think it would happen to me. It's terrifying knowing that you can be framed for a murder, and there's not a damn thing you can do about it."

"Let me help, Melanie! Tell me what I can do?"

"There's nothing you can do…the only person who could help, who can help, won't!"

"Huh, who?"

"Never mind, it doesn't matter. There is something you can do for me, though."

"Okay, name it!"

"I need you to talk to Toni. I need you to try and convince him to come see me. Everyone has been by to see me, even Josh! But Toni, nope! And I don't know if he's convinced himself that I murdered his ex-boyfriend or what, but I need him to know the truth. I have to see him before I get bussed out of here."

"Yeah, sure, I'll see what I can do. But you're not going anywhere, Melanie. We're going to get you out of here."

"I doubt it! But thank you for the…kind words. Is there anything else?"

Now, this was my chance to tell Melanie about Ms. Bailey's condition, but instead, I froze and said,

"No…no, that's it. I will give Toni your message."

I couldn't do it. I couldn't look Melanie in her already sad eyes and tell her that Ms. Bailey was dying from heart disease. And maybe that was selfish of me because I couldn't deal with the effects that telling her would cause. I figured Melanie needed every bit of fighting strength she had left to focus on getting out, and I thought that once she was free, we could face whatever challenges came next together. But that was a week ago, and she was still sitting in there. It seemed that everything we were trying was failing. The lawyer Melanie had, I heard, was a complete idiot, and it didn't seem like he was trying much of anything to get her out. Melanie was right, it had been months since James's death, and people were ready to close the case, desperate to find Justice no matter whose face was on the newspaper.

Well, back to graduation, it was almost 11:45 A.M., time for all of the seniors to march outside to the football field where our ceremony was taking place. And all you could see down the hall was endless black caps and gowns. We each huddled together as we waited for our cues. I was standing alone until I wasn't when Josh and Crystal interrupted me as they approached.

"Hey, this is wild, right?" Josh asked.

"Man, I'm just ready to get this over with and never see inside these walls again!"

"Oh, come on, Jesuse, I know you're going to miss it at least a little bit. The smell of mini weenies and mashed potatoes cooking in the cafeteria? The crowd of freshman by your locker, and oh yeah, fifth period with Ms. Bloom?" Crystal teased.

I felt her gaze, her smile, as she grabbed onto my soul, just for a moment. I smiled back and then said,

"Nah, not even fifth period with the wicked witch of the west. Though lately, she has been acting kind of off. Have you noticed?"

"What do you mean?" Crystal asked.

"I don't know, after visiting Melanie, she said something that got me thinking."

"Like what?"

"Wait, you visited Melanie?" Josh blurted out.

"Yes, why?"

"Well, did she anything…about me?" Josh demanded.

"No, only that you went and saw her. Why?"

While Josh and I were playing detective, we didn't notice our conversation was about to be rudely interjected by no one other than,

"Joshy, my boy! I see that you've finally made a full recovery?"

"What are you doing here, Biscuit?" Crystal asked.

"Well, isn't it obvious? I'm graduating with my class!"

"Well, why don't you go stand over there?" Crystal pointed.

"Oh, how cute! Joshy, are you having your little girlfriend fight your battles for you now? Listen, I don't know if you guys got the memo, but high school is over. We're stepping into the real world now. And in the real world, men don't need their little girlfriends to fight their battles for them, or their pretty boyfriends either."

"Okay, Biscuit. I'm here! I'm standing right in front of you. You wanna fight, let's fight! But this time, keep your body-guards out of it. This is between you and me."

"Josh, stop!" Crystal begged.

We stood still surrounded by black caps and gowns, yet it felt like we were the only people in the room. Josh and Biscuit stood face-to-face, ready to start World War Three. Crystal then found herself getting caught in the middle trying to separate the two of them, and that's when my instincts kicked in full force. Biscuit has always been a wild card; you can never really know what's going on through that fucked up brain of his. Before I could suit up for battle, Biscuit calmly took a step back, smiled, and said,

"Take a chill pill, guys! I'm not going to fight anyone today. The way I see it, I have the next four years to plan the perfect punishment for my boy Joshy here."

"What the hell have you been snorting? After today, I don't plan on seeing your ass ever again."

"Damn! I must have beat short-term memory loss into you! Sad but, no worries, allow me to remind you. Uh, we both got accepted into the same college program! Which was amazing news for me, but not so good for you since it also means that you'll be seeing a lot more of me for the next four years! Unless fear sets in again, and you decided to take classes online underneath your mama's mattress?"

"You really think that I'm scared of you? Trust me; I'm far from it! It took five of you to almost kill me! But look at me now; I'm smiling and feeling better than ever! I do wonder, though, if you've lost your touch, you know, since Brenden? I mean, back then, you did your own dirty work. I guess throughout the years, it's you who's turned into a coward. Because between you and me, I don't need a crew to help take you down. I'll do that all by myself!"

"Really?"

"Yes! Really! We both might be joining the same Criminal Justice program, but only one of us will end up with a badge. I will spend every day doing whatever I can to make sure that you pay for your crimes. And I won't rest until your ass is behind bars begging ME to see another sunset."

Before I could break up their little dance of intimidation, we were interrupted by a couple of our teachers, one being Ms. Bloom, as she tried to move us along down the hallway.

"Hey guys, we're going to be heading out to the field soon. So, I need you to go stand with your assigned groups, please."

"Oh, Ms. Bloom, so good to see you! I was just stopping by to wish everyone here farewell. I'm gonna miss these guys, except for Josh, though. It looks like he and I are on our way to becoming partners in crime. Speaking of crime, do you know if the police ever caught James's real killer?"

The animosity between Biscuit and Ms. Bloom was heavy! The look on Ms. Blooms face as Biscuit wickedly smiled before walking away scared even me! Then after she reminded us once more to get into our groups, we slowly walked away as Josh blurted out in a whisper,

"Oh my God, did you just see that?"

"See what, Josh?" Crystal asked.

"The look on her face!" Josh replied.

"Whose face?"

"Ms. Bloom! I think she did it, and Biscuit somehow knows. But, the way she just looked at him, come on!"

"Josh, I think you're being dramatic. Just get in line! It's graduation day, for crying out loud. Can we just try to pretend for the next hour that our lives are normal?"

I walked away, leaving Crystal and Josh to hash out their differences. While I was making my way towards my group, I ran into Toni. He was having a breakdown in front of Principal Settle. I tried to catch his attention as I slowly walked by.

But he was too distraught to notice me. So I stalled and took baby steps while eavesdropping.

"What does it matter if I wear a gown underneath another gown? Who's going to see it?" Toni asked.

"I can see it, Toni. And you know the rules."

"What rules? I'm not a student here anymore. The only thing I'm going to do is march outside, sit and wait for you to hand me my diploma! Then I'm gone! You can't turn a blind eye for an hour or two?"

"It's not just about me, Toni. We have a reputation to uphold. There are parents, families outside waiting to watch their loved ones graduate. How's it going to look to them if you go out there and turn it into a joke?"

"A joke? Is that what you think of me, of who I am? My family is one of those families outside waiting to watch their loved one, me, graduate! It was never my intention to make people laugh with my style of clothing. But it's part of who I am. It's what makes me, me! And when you care more about someone's closed-minded opinions rather than the person you're trying to hide from the world, you play a part in that ignorance. I'm sorry but, I cleaned out my locker, and I won't dare ask my mom and dad to drive me home to change into clothes that will appease you or anyone else. If you don't want me to walk across that stage, if you want to take that right away from me, then you can be the one to tell my family the reason why they won't be able to watch their loved one graduate today!"

Damn! He was not playing at all. And I was running out of time. Three different teachers told me to take my place in line already. And though I so badly wanted to see how things would have played out, I told myself I'd wait and find out later. As I got in line with my group, I turned around one last time and saw Toni getting in line as well. So I figured whatever he said worked in his favor, and I left the rest to be a mystery.

I COULDN'T believe that woman; she just couldn't give it a rest! And I meant what I said, if Bitch Settle didn't want me to walk across the stage because of what I was wearing underneath my gown, then she could be the one to tell my parents that, not me. But of course, no one wants that kind of responsibility, and she didn't say a word after that! I figured she wouldn't. I had dealt with enough shit recently, and I didn't even have the patience to entertain Principal Settle. The last couple of months leading up to graduation, it's transformed me in ways I never imagined possible. And when it was time to walk outside, I couldn't help but think about Melanie and the fact that she wasn't there with us.

But as our senior class got lined up and ready to march, we headed down the stairs and out the double doors and could suddenly hear the graduation wedding song playing in the distance. Yes! That song, honey! As we continued marching toward the field, I felt a mix of emotions. I was nervous, excited. My heart was racing as I looked up at my family in the bleachers. I was ready! But then there was another part of me, a dark, angry side! And although it was the happiest, fullest day of my life, I couldn't help feeling incredibly alone. There's a lot I haven't told you yet, about what happened to me during the weeks leading up to graduation. Before I go ahead unravel that nightmare, I'd like to tell you about the visit I had with Melanie. I honestly wasn't sure if I would ever see her again. I don't know why, but I think part of me blamed her for my unhappiness.

It took Jesuse to convince me to finally visit Melanie. I think it was three or four days before graduation. I had been dealing with so much personally, mentally, and along with school, I just never found the time. Okay, excuses. I could have made the time, but I didn't know what to believe. Part of me knew that Melanie would never hurt James, not like that. But the other part of me remembered the conversations and their arguments, and I guess I just went along with what everyone around me was saying. That it's always the quiet ones, the nice ones, the person you would never expect. Maybe I wasn't strong enough to think for myself, to know my friend, to know her heart. And although my body was at graduation, sitting with my peers, my mind was back at the jail, sitting solo across from Melanie. The glass separated us, but I was immediately surprised at how well she looked. Maybe I was partly jealous that she seemed to be doing better in there than I was out here. Melanie just looked at me and smiled in her grey sweatsuit. Then after an entire minute of emotionally smiling at one another, Melanie said,

"So what took you so long? I was starting to think that you hated me."

"Hate you?" I asked.

"Toni, you're the only person who hasn't come by to see me. Even Josh managed to get a visit in, even though he was mostly here for his own selfish reasons."

"I'm sorry...I know I should have come by sooner, but... I couldn't."

"Wait, do you really believe…"

"No, not at first. But then I started thinking about that night. And how you disappeared into the woods like you was, *Weekend at Bernie's*. I mean, you were standing right next to Gabrielle, and then you weren't. Plus, you and James were fighting almost every time you saw each other."

"Fighting is one thing, but killing? And Toni, we fought because I was protecting you! I'm your best friend. No matter how I may have felt about James, I could never do something like that. What's been going on with you?"

"What do you mean?"

"Even if, at your core, you believed I did it, I don't think that would be enough to keep you from visiting me. Something else is going on with you."

I tried not to show it. I didn't want Melanie to know what was weighing on my spirit. I felt ashamed, embarrassed. But when I lifted my right arm to rub the back of my head, I mistakenly revealed a large bruise on my inner forearm. Immediately I tried to pull my arm down before she could notice, but Melanie's got quick eyes, and she saw it immediately. I watched as her eyebrows rose and her mouth loosened. I then waited for her to say,

"Toni, what's that on your arm?"

"It's nothing! I-I slipped on the wet floor and fell… it's nothing."

"Michael? Did he do this to you? He did, didn't he?"

I couldn't lie. As much as I wanted to, my expression gave the truth away. I couldn't even look Melanie in the eye anymore as I turned away in shame.

"This is why you didn't want to see me, isn't it? How long?"

"How long what?" I asked.

"How long...how often is this happening? I swear if I weren't in here, I'd kill him myself!"

"See, Melanie! When you go and say things like that, how am I not supposed to believe that you mean it?"

"I didn't...I shouldn't have said that. *It was a figure of speech to those listening in on the conversation.* Look, I'd hurt anyone who puts hands on the people I love, but that's as far as I'd go. So why didn't you tell me this was happening? And Michael? I'm surprised because he seems like such a nice person!"

"Well, it's like I said, Melanie. It's always the nice and quiet ones that surprise you the most. And I didn't tell you because it's embarrassing! How is it even possible that I'd go from a bad relationship to worse? I don't understand; I'm a good person! I'm kind, thoughtful, caring. So why can't I get some of that love back? I don't ask for a lot, I would be happy just to get a quarter of what I give, but I don't even get that. And the only conclusion that I've come up with is that I'm probably not as good of a person as I think I am, or maybe I'm undeserving of kindness!"

"No, that's not true! Don't you dare think that you don't deserve the same amount of love you give! Hell, you deserve double, triple, of what you put into the world."

"If that's true, then why does this keep happening to me, huh? And we thought James was bad, but he had nothing on Michael! The first time I went through this when I was with James, I got through it because I had you! But without you, I don't think I'll be able to survive another relationship like this and still be the same person. I'm watching myself slowly turn into something I don't like. It's crazy, right before graduation, the time where we are supposed to be more sure of ourselves; I'm completely lost!"

"Well, I know you! I know that you're so much stronger than you realize. The kindhearted, vivacious, joyful person who befriended me at the beginning of senior year is still in there! It is your core! I'm learning that life has a way of testing us to our breaking point, but you should remember who you are through it all! Remember that you are Toni Fabulous Fucking Broussard, and you don't follow any pronouns or fashion statements. Instead, you lead as your own individual, a bright and colorful rarity...

"People will come along and try to break you because rare in this world is feared, misunderstood, and forced into formation. Don't let this guy or anyone take your rareness, your specialness, away from you. Because without that, you end up falling into line with the rest of the followers. Be a leader, and remember that you don't need me to remind you of how strong you are...

"And if you need to fight back to free yourself, then you put up your deuces and fight! You don't need anyone in your life who can't respect you, your mind, and your body! And maybe that is your test; learning to love yourself so much that you won't even let anyone look at your sideways. Because it's they who are lost, not you."

We were just about in tears. I was so moved by what Melanie said that I carried it with me throughout the week. I think it's easy to hear something in a moment, to get your fix of encouragement. But after a while, it starts to wear off, and you need another dose to get you back into shape, which is why I'm ashamed to admit that I started getting encouragement elsewhere. It became the only way to cloud out the arguments, fights, and depression. The saddest part of Michael and I's relationship was that we didn't even have a honeymoon phase! Instead, we dove right into the sex and drama. I couldn't see it at first until Melanie mentioned it, but I think I was so desperate to have love again that I stopped loving myself in the process.

I spent most of my time during graduation ceremony in a daze. When I was finally able to snap out of my memories and take a moment to smell the freshly cut grass and wind blowing through my cap, I think I may have smiled for a brief second. Soon after the assistant principal called my name, I found myself walking across the stage and waving at my family like I was in a beauty pageant after accepting my diploma. And as I took a moment to mentally photograph my graduating class cheering before me, I looked for Melanie, knowing damn well she wasn't out there. But I missed her so much that I looked for her anyway. I missed her being out in the real world with me; I missed the laughs and talks in the cafeteria. I missed everything! On my way back to my seat, I saw Gabrielle. I waved, and she waved back with a smile.

OH, TONI, my sweet Toni! I didn't realize how much I would miss him, my friends, and the look and feel of old paint on the walls and stairwells until I was saying my goodbyes. The last couple of months leading up to graduation were a total mess, I think, for everyone. I found myself growing closer to people I never in a million years imagined that I would. Crystal and I became strangely close, of all people, Crystal! I sat there at graduation with my heart still broken, with dying butterflies in my stomach, and a sudden drop in body temperature. I often found myself gazing up at the top of the bleachers, eagerly waiting for Melanie to rush down with her hand in the air saying, wait, I'm here!

But even wishing for a miracle, I knew that Melanie would never come. And it's crazy how even with a broken heart, I managed to love her still. My lingering love for Melanie was the very reason why I needed to move on, and I did move on! Yet, I still found myself holding on to her. I think I visited Melanie at the county jail more than anyone else, including Renee. Which was why I promised myself that the next time I saw Melanie, would be my last. It was about a week before graduation.

I remember the day well because of the conversation that Melanie and I had. A large part of me wasn't ready to give her up, but the other was ready to start a new chapter. As I went to sit down right across from Melanie, she had this smile that almost brought me to tears. I think part of it was guilt because I knew that I was there to say goodbye. I felt her smile touch me to my core. Then as I got comfortable in my seat and nervously smiled back, I said,

"Wow! Jail really has grown on you!"

"I see you got jokes!" Melanie grinned.

"No, I'm serious! I mean, most people have a look of defeat, but you are oddly glowing."

"There's nothing odd about that. You're the reason why I

smile. Every time I see you, you give me hope. Your glow is what's been keeping me alive in here."

Then she goes and says something like that! Which made it that much more difficult for me to say,

"That's sweet, Melanie but, that's the reason why I came to see you today. I don't…I can't. Today will be the last day that you see me. I can't keep doing this to myself. I mean, I have college. There's a lot that I have to get ready for, and I need to have a clear mind. But more importantly, I need to move on with my life… I want to!"

"Where is this coming from?"

"It's coming from me, Melanie! As long as I keep showing up, I'm giving you a piece of myself that, frankly, I don't think you deserve. I'm telling you that there's still a chance for us when there isn't! I've finally accepted the truth, so should you!"

"What truth?"

"That you love her!"

There was silence as I waited for Melanie to rebuttal my argument, but she didn't, and that's when I knew.

"I know that she had something to do with this, and yet you're still in here! I can't compete with that kind of love!"

"There's no competition, Gabrielle. There never was! If I have to spend the rest of my life proving that you, I will! You and I, we're supposed to be together!"

"Supposed? I'm strongly beginning to hate that word. Because if you were supposed to be with her and me, who would you choose? If there were no rules, if it was okay by society to be with her, who would you choose?"

Her pause and lingering gaze said everything! The fact

that she didn't immediately choose me not only broke off another piece of my heart, but it pissed me off!

"It's okay, I'm with Justin now anyway, and we're getting married, so…"

"Wait, what! Are you serious?"

"Yes! He proposed to me a couple of days ago, and I said, yes!"

"What did he propose with…a purple ring pop?" Melanie jokingly asked.

"Actually, it was green, my favorite color!" I replied sarcastically.

"Seriously, Gabrielle? Do you really expect me to believe that? How could you even think about getting engaged to someone else when you know that you're still in love with me? Out of everyone I know, you're the person who's visited me the most. How can you not call that love?"

Melanie was right. I wasn't over her, which was the very reason why I needed to stop seeing her. I mean, when I got back with Justin, life was so much easier. I felt like I no longer had to fight a losing battle with my dad. Like I could finally breathe again. And Melanie would have been worth fighting for if only she would have chosen me.

"You're right, Melanie. I do love you! But it doesn't matter because I'm supposed to be with Justin."

And just like that, our conversation was over. It wasn't easy, leaving Melanie behind. But I knew it was the right thing to do. It was what I had to do! And so, as I sat there in my seat at graduation waiting for them to call my name, I put on a smile while glaring in Crystal's direction. I then graciously waved as I eagerly waited to begin the new chapters of my life.

GABRIELLE was always so humble and sweet. I never expected that we'd end our senior year as friends. So much has changed in the year, and yet, so much has remained the same. I watched Josh grow from a self-centered insecure boy to this caring and brave man. Sure, he still had a long way to go, but I felt proud to call him my friend again. When Josh and I were younger, I couldn't imagine myself without him. I just knew that he was the only guy for me; that was until I met Jesuse. You think you know what direction love is taking you until one day it blindsides you into a corner, forcing you to choose between the familiar and unfamiliar. Gabrielle and I shared that similar feeling, although we were on opposite ends of the triangle. I was caught in the middle trying to decide between two boys while Gabrielle was on the end of waiting to be chosen.

I think, in a way, we all want to be chosen by someone. To know and feel what it is like, not to wonder, but to know without a doubt that you are the ONE. So when Gabrielle came around asking me for advice, I told her the only thing I could think to say at the time, that the heart is more complex than we realize. That it's not impossible to be in love with more than one person at the same time. And right when I said it, I realized that I was talking about myself. Josh has tried almost everything under the sun to get back with me, including his new obsessive compulsion to solve James's murder. I would have been an idiot if I didn't believe for a second that I was partly the reason for his sudden revelation to be a better person. Honestly, I didn't care where his inspiration came from; I was glad to see him changing for the better. I wasn't sure how long it would last, but I was hopeful for the best.

Then one day, Gabrielle asked me a question, one that had never crossed my mind. She asked if I had to choose between Josh and Jesuse, who would I choose and why! Without hesitation, I said Jesuse. But when it came down to me explaining the why, I was conflicted again. It wasn't until I was sitting there at graduation, watching Jesuse walk across the stage, taking a moment to find me in the crowd and smile, that I knew! I felt tears of joy and sadness streaming down my face because I thought that once the ceremony was over, we'd never see each other again. Right at that moment, I decided that I would tell him how I felt. I was ready! When it was finally time for me to walk across the stage, turning my tassel from right to left, I became ecstatic. I finally did it! But then suddenly, I felt wretched as I remembered a conversation I had with my parents two weeks prior.

It was an exhilarating day for me; I hadn't yet told anyone that I got accepted into the Fashion Institute of Technology in New York City. I didn't even think about applying to any colleges until Josh brought it up at James's wake. Since then, I'd been getting back into drawing. It was exciting, finally feeling like I had a purpose, something that was mine and unique to look forward to instead of a bunch of pointless drama. Though, when I went to share the good news with my parents one evening over dinner, they weren't as thrilled.

"New York? Why do you need to go to New York?" My mother asked.

"Because it's one of the best cities in the country to go to for fashion design! What am I supposed to do here in Indiana?"

"There are plenty of schools right here. You could go to school in Indianapolis even. That way, your father and I could still see you on the weekends. We will never see you if you move to New York. You don't even know anybody out there! Anything could happen to you."

"Anything could happen to me here too! Mom, Dad, this is my dream. It's something I'm really good at! Why can't you guys support me?"

"It's not that we don't support you, honey. We just want what's best for you. I worry that choosing this career path will leave you disappointed and BROKE! The fashion world is tough to break into, and there's so much competition in the bigger cities. Why don't you pick something more practical? Something you could succeed at, something that will pay the bills? I mean, Crystal, do you want to become a starving artist?"

"No, mom... you're right. I should just sit up under you all day talking about breast and butt implants! God! You really don't believe in me, do you?"

"We do believe in you, Crystal, but you're our only kid! Your dad is almost 60, and sometimes he acts like he can't tell up from down or left from right."

"Honey! You do realize that I'm still sitting in the room?"

My father took offense while mother just fanned him away and continued,

"It would just be a shame if you wasted your life away on a dream instead of pursuing an actual career! Most people spend their entire lives chasing a dream. Why don't you go

into Social Work? Lord knows we need a lot more good social workers around here."

There was nothing I could say. I allowed doubt to con-
sume me into believing that I wasn't as talented as I thought.
That maybe I didn't have what it would take to succeed. Because if my own parents didn't believe in me, how could I
even begin to believe in myself? After that conversation, I
withdrew my application and applied to a local college for
general education. I wasn't sure what else I wanted to do, and
I sure as hell wasn't going to let my mom choose my major
for me. I just needed more time to figure out what I could do
that would be more...*practical*. What my mom said was true
though, my dad was starting to decline in his memory. He
was in his late sixties, after all. I began feeling like it would be
selfish of me to leave them alone. So, I figured, heck, I'm still
young. New York will always be there when I'm ready, right?

Well, that's what I told myself as I accepted my diploma
from Principal Settle. The rest of the ceremony went by fast
after that. I think we were all just ready to leave until it was
finally time to go. I caught up with Gabrielle and Jesuse after the ceremony. It was an emotional time; all the seniors
were back inside the school huddled in the hallway, saying
their goodbyes, a much different feeling from before when
we first arrived. Before I said goodbye to Gabrielle, we exchanged numbers and promised each other that we'd keep in
touch. Not even a minute later, Jesuse walked up wearing the
biggest smile on his face. I was ready to tell him how I felt.
It was now or never, I thought. Before I could muster up the

courage, Renee walked up out of nowhere as she clung onto Jesuse with a smile. I froze. I was confused.

"Hey! What's going on here?" I asked nervously.

"Oh, yeah, Renee and I...we uh, we decided to give things another shot," Jesuse replied.

"Wow! Since when?"

Forget being hurt and confused. I was furious! Then Renee interrupted,

"It was right around the time when Ms. Bailey got sick, and with the whole Melanie situation, it just felt like both our worlds were falling apart. So, I promised Jesuse I'd be there for him while you were taking care of Josh."

Taking care of Josh? That Bitch! I saw exactly what she was doing, but I wasn't going to let old habits resurface and get the best of me. Instead, I ignored Renee and said to Jesuse,

"I was giving you space...to heal! Which is what I thought you needed? A little warning would have been nice, but I'm learning that with you, such a thing is impossible."

Jesuse just stood there with his head held down, mute! Then Renee interrupted again,

"Crystal, let's not fight. I mean, you got your guy, and I have mine. So maybe the four of us could even do a double date sometime?"

"Sure, Renee. Let's! Anyway, Jesuse, I have to go find my parents, but you two, I hope it works out this time around."

Not! Inside I wished that they'd break up as soon as the next day. And seeing Jesuse with Renee only confirmed my feelings for him. I didn't care anymore about what my parents would think or say or that Jesuse and I came from different racial backgrounds. What mattered most was the heartbreak

I felt as I reached in and gave Jesuse the tightest hug, goodbye. I hated feeling jealous over him. I hated feeling jealous, period. I'm sure if I ever saw Josh with another girl, I'd be jealous over him too. I think it was my twisted way of wanting to be chosen even if the person was someone I no longer wanted. But Jesuse, he was the boy I wanted, the only boy, and all I could do at that moment was swallow my pride, smile, and walk away, walk away from him, one last time.

I DON'T KNOW what to say. I know it probably doesn't make any sense, but Renee really was there for me when I needed someone the most. Even after the way I treated her, after leaving her hot and dry, she came back! And yeah, watching Crystal clean up after Josh 24/7 did piss me off a little. I couldn't show it. But I knew I'd never compare to him. I knew that Josh would come included in the package if Crystal and I were to ever be together. But with Renee, there was no Josh, no baggage or anything else; it was just her! Since my mom's been gone, I tried to take life more seriously. I no longer had her wisdom to protect me, to guide me; so, I needed to be mother and father to myself and make better choices. Renee was familiar and, in some ways, reminded me of my mother, which was comforting. Before Renee and I got back together, I started thinking about the conversation Crystal and I shared about dating and race. Sure, I fought her on it, explaining how the less than one inch of skin that covers our body shouldn't make a difference, but then I wondered, maybe it does!

Renee and I share the same melanin, and with that also came our shared culture and struggle. Crystal would never get that; she would never understand it, so I thought. I just knew that I needed to choose someone who'd understand me, my pain, and not run from it. How could I make Crystal understand when she never thought to ask? I didn't understand how people from different racial backgrounds could be in a relationship if they were too afraid to learn about each other's struggles. With Renee, I knew that would never be an issue. And maybe that's why a lot of people prefer to date within their race. But if we all did that, how would we ever learn to come together, truly? How would we learn about each other? I guess that's why I chose Renee; it was easier that way.

Speaking of Renee, right before we were about to say goodbye to our second home of four years, Toni approached. He skipped his way over in a hurry and quickly greeted Renee, then pulled me to the side. The matter seemed urgent, so I gave Toni my undivided attention.

"I hate to ask again, but I ran out of pills last week. I was hoping I could come by later and get some more off of you?"

"Toni, no! I told you that the last time was going to be it! You don't need to get yourself addicted to that shit. Besides, after today, I'm done dealing."

"Wow, so that's it? You had no problem taking my money when you needed it, and now that you don't, all of a sudden, I have an addiction? I need those pills, Jesuse, they…that shit, helps me deal with my shit! And if you won't sell to me, I'll find someone else who will."

I hesitated. I felt terrible. What was supposed to be a one-time thing became a weekly transaction because, sad to say, I needed the money. Toni has been crying out for help, but I ignored that cry to keep my pockets full. Toni begged me one last time to help him out as we stood off to the side, with Renee folding her arms in the distance. I just looked at Toni and said,

"I'm sorry! I really am Toni, but I can't...I won't. You need to talk to someone, get some help. Hell, talk to me. I'm not going anywhere! But you don't need this!"

Before I could finish talking, Toni stormed away. He didn't even say goodbye to Renee as she rushed up, confused.

"What's going on with Toni?"

"I don't know..." I replied.

"What do you mean you don't know? I've never seen him like that before. What did you say to him?"

"I didn't say anything. I just...listen, I need to do something. I promise I'll call you later, but I have to go."

I couldn't tell Renee the truth. I couldn't tell anyone that I was back dealing. That is why I promised myself that if I made it to graduation, I'd get out, no more dealing. I had one last thing to do in order to be free, one last promise to fulfill. After Renee and I parted, I looked for Ms. Bailey to tell her not to wait up for me. Poor Ms. B, she tried not to show it, but I could tell she was struggling. Her eyes were heavy, almost lifeless. But with a smile, she fought on. I offered to drive her home, in her car, of course. But Ms. Bailey just stared, grabbed my cheeks with both her hands and said,

"Jesuse, I might be dying tomorrow, but I'm alive today. I can drive myself around the corner. Don't worry. I'll see you when you get back."

Her voice was so soft and calm as if she had made peace with what was to come. I couldn't help but get a little emotional. We suffered so much loss in one year; I suffered! And

I wondered, what was the point of so much suffering? For the amount of laughter and joy we experience each year, it feels like the scales favor sadness. Like for every good day on Earth, you gotta get through one hundred more bad days just to get another perfect day. Well, as I got ready to say good-bye to 720 days of memories, I walked past familiar faces, old teachers, and even my freshman year English teacher Mrs. Sharp. She just smiled and waved; I could feel how proud she was. Oh, and don't tell anybody this but, I even went past my locker, just to take in the memories of old conversations, jokes, even fights between me and, you know who.

I didn't think I'd miss the place. But as I made my way outside and took a look at the brick walls that made up Lee Wallace High and the black and yellow paint that covered it, the moment became bittersweet. That was until my new pal startled me back into reality!

"Hey man, you're not about to cry, are you?" Josh teased.

"Dammit, Josh! You almost gave me a… You fuckin scared me!"

"Dude, you know I wasn't gonna leave without saying goodbye."

"What are you talking about? I'm sure you'll still be around bugging the hell out of me every other day."

"Yeah, maybe on the weekends?"

"Whatever! Hey, can I get a ride from you? I was going to take the bus, but…"

"Yeah, sure, just let me find my parents and tell them I'm leaving. If they can stop fighting for two minutes, I'll take you wherever you need to go. Where are you going?"

"Oh uhm, across town near the old mall. I have an uh, an interview."

"You have a job interview at the dead mall? The same day of graduation?"

"Yeah..."

"There's like two stores in there! An interview where?"

"Josh, can you give me a ride or not?"

"Yes! Jeez, secrete agent, just wait here. I'll be right back."

Josh glared at me with skepticism before he jogged away. I waited outside for ten minutes before he came back and told me he was ready to go. Josh convinced his parents to let him use his mom's car to drive me across town. Josh's parents reminded me of him and Crystal. For two people who were supposed to be divorcing, they sure did spend a lot of time together. Maybe it's a cultural thing. I had no idea. I couldn't worry about that when I was about to make the biggest decision of my life. While Josh and I were on our way, he started grilling me right when I was in the process of removing my cap and gown. I had a small backpack with me where I stored my belongings. I think Josh knew what I was up to, which is why he wouldn't shut up. But I made up my mind. And when my mind is made, there's no stopping me!

When we finally arrived at the mall, Josh parked in front of the abandoned clock store and suddenly refused to let me out by activating the child lock on the doors.

"Josh, unlock the fucking door!"

"No, Jesuse! I'm not going to let you do this. It's still daylight, for crying out loud."

"I don't know what you're talking about, but you're about to make me late!"

"Dammit, man, you don't need to lie to me. I know you!"

"Josh! Unlock the door! Don't make me reach over and unlock it myself."

We sat in the car staring at each other. I held on tight to my bag, ready to go, and I watched while Josh hesitated to unlock the door. He then took a deep breath and said to me,

"Fine! You wanna ruin your life and swap prison stories with Melanie, go right ahead. I won't stop you."

As soon as I heard the click in the door, I bolted. I spent every month leading up to this moment coaching myself, preparing myself for battle. Seconds later, I heard tires screeching from behind me as Josh sped off. Then as I made my way closer to the building, I hid and waited to make sure that Josh was gone before I diverted away from the mall. This particular part of town was called Old Town. There were many abandoned buildings and a railroad track a couple of blocks away, where I was headed. New Fernando told me she would deliver old Fernando to me by the train tracks right at 2 o'clock. Clever thinking because every day at 2 P.M., a train comes that takes five to seven minutes to pass. And that was my window!

While waiting, I took my bag and placed it next to an abandoned house nearby. Same at graduation. I knew I couldn't bring my bag that had a Glock 17 hidden inside into the building. So, I hid my bag inside one of the bushes near the side of the school when security wasn't looking and prayed like hell that no one would find it. I was going to need every bit of gun powder I had for the fight that was before me. Then as I stood near the train tracks, I kept my eyes and ears peeled, waiting for Fernando to sneak up and try and get the drop on me. But I stayed focused, pointing my gun in whatever direction the wind would take me. Then minutes after my watch read 2 P.M., I began thinking that maybe I was being set up. The train hadn't even passed yet. It's like whatever could go wrong did go wrong! That was until I heard the driest voice say in the slimmest way possible,

"Que haces aqui, amigo?"

Fuck! It was Fernando! The son of a bitch startled me as he appeared out of nowhere. He was just a few feet away. Seconds later, I heard the bells ringing as the train made its way in front of us. Then as Fernando slowly walked closer and the train got louder, I heard him say,

"Now, what are you gonna do with that? Huh?"

Before I opened my mouth, I stared Fernando down as I watched him reach behind his pocket, waiting to draw out his weapon. I could feel the humming of the wheels as the train went by vibrating through my body. Fernando just stood there, trying to talk me down as he kept his one hand pressed behind his back, waiting to make his move. I was ready! I had the drop on him, all I had to do was pull the trigger, but instead, I became frozen with fear and doubt. My inner mother's voice was trying to force me out of making a wrong decision. But the Jesue in me needed revenge! And when Fernando looked like he was about to make a move, I shouted,

"You took the person I loved most in this world, the only family I had left; you snatched her out of my life like she was nothing! Her life wasn't yours to take, Fernando! She...she was already dying! And you stole that time, the time that I had left to say goodbye. You robbed me of it! So now it's time for me to steal something from you!"

"Well, it's like you said, Jesuse, she was dying anyway. So, what's the big deal?"

That's when I immediately saw red! I felt my face go from warm to blistering within a matter of seconds. My heart was beating, no, pounding through my chest as I tried to wrap my mind around Fernando's psychotic mind. In doing so, I let my guard down out of weakness, and with it, my arm slightly as well. Fernando then had the drop on me. I quickly re-tightened my pasture while re-aiming my gun directly between his hazel-colored eyes. The train beside us was blowing wind in our direction, going about 25 miles per hour. I was ready to turn his lights out for good; I wanted to see blood! Then out of nowhere, I could see over Fernando's shoulder, Josh sneaking his ass down the hill.

What the hell is he doing, I asked myself. I just prayed that Josh wouldn't make the situation worse or get himself caught and shot. Fernando quickly took advantage of yet another weak moment as he rushed up and head-butted me, causing me to lose my balance, and then kneed me to the ground. Soon after, Fernando positioned himself on top of me, I squirmed around, reaching for my gun, but Fernando had already tossed it out of reach. That was it. I could see the end! As Fernando pressed his gun on top of my forehead, I saw my life flashing before my eyes. Everything was happening so fast that I just closed my eyes and waited for Fernando to pull the trigger. Then out of nowhere, I heard,

"Hey! Let him go!"

I opened my eyes, and I could see Josh standing in front of us, pointing my gun at Fernando's head. Fernando kept his hold on me, pressing his gun deeper into my skin as he looked at Josh and said,

"Who the fuck are you?"

"Josh, get out of here! Now's not the time to play good cop!" I shouted.

"I'm not going anywhere until he lets you go!"

"Fine! I don't have time for this bullshit!"

Fernando then turned back towards me and added,

"Jesuse, tell your mother hello for me, will you?"

I squeezed my eyes tight while listening to the cocking of Fernando's gun, then out of nowhere I heard the sounds, BANG! BANG! POP! The aftershock of gunfire carried away with the passing train. I looked down at myself, and I was shaking. My chest was covered in blood, so much blood! I couldn't breathe, I couldn't smell, I couldn't hear, I couldn't even move. Josh then rushed towards me hysterically, and I could barely hear him say,

"I'm sorry! I'm so sorry. I didn't mean to…"

"Am I dead?" I asked.

"What!"

The look on Josh's face after I said that was comical. He examined me from head to torso, looked at me again, and said,

"Dude, I was apologizing for splattering Fernando's blood all over your face. You look like fucking Bloody Mary's baby!"

"Fernando?" I asked.

"Yeah, I think I killed him!"

"NO...I killed Fernando! You just shot him in the leg a couple of times!"

Josh turned around, screaming like a five-year-old girl, while I was crying on the inside! We had no idea what was going on. It wasn't until she stepped into view that I began piecing it all together. The unspoken one whose name I shall never know, the one who set up this meeting where I was supposed to get my revenge when instead, she ended up being the one to save me. All I could think was that I failed again. I sat up and glared over at Fernando's body, making my way to his skull that had blood oozing out from the side.

"I don't understand. This was supposed to be my fight!" I replied.

"This was never just your fight, Jesuse. Fernando took something from me too! I just needed to use you as a distraction. I knew that it was the only way he'd let his guard down."

"But I wanted to avenge my mother! It was supposed to be me!"

"Does it really matter who did it? And trust me, you don't want that kind of blood on your hands. You're young; you have your whole life ahead of you. And I know that your mother would want you to do something with it!"

I slowly got up from the ground after taking a hand from Josh. I then used the inside of my shirt to wipe as much blood off my face as possible before saying,

"I'm done dealing... I'm out!"

She then smiled and said,

"I know! This life, it was never meant for you, Jesuse. Now go! I never want to see or hear about you in the streets again. We'll take care of the rest from here."

Walking towards us was Manny and another guy from my old crew. So naturally, Josh and I were skeptical. We didn't believe she would just let us walk away untouched. But as we slowly started to walk away, with our lives still intact, we began to question, why?

"Damn, is she really going to let us walk away like that? And can you just quit the business whenever you want? I thought that once you were in, you were in, for life."

"I don't know. Maybe she'll shoot us in our backs right when we hit the corner. Which is why we should probably move a little faster."

Josh and I picked up the pace while looking back every five seconds. Then right before I followed Josh around the corner, I looked back again and saw her smiling back at me. It was the most confusing ten seconds of my life. I felt like I was in the middle of the Twilight Zone. But we made it around the corner, untouched and alive! We took a minute to sit on the porch and catch our breaths at the abandoned house where I kept my bag.

"Damn, that was close!" Josh said while panting.

"What the hell were you thinking? You could have gotten yourself killed!" I shouted.

"I wasn't going to let you do this alone! You saved my life. I owed you at least that much."

"You don't owe me anything! And the legs, bro; what the hell? I hope they give you extra shooting lessons before they release you out on the streets."

"Shut up!"

Josh and I were laughing so hard at his horrible aiming skills that I felt like I was getting a charley horse in the stomach! Oh, it was painful but good! I finally felt a sense of relief, like the weight I was carrying was suddenly lifted. Josh then asked,

"Hey, the lady back there, are you guys related or something?"

"What? Hell no! I don't even know her name. Why do you ask?"

"I don't know, I just thought, well, never mind! It's a silly question, I guess."

"Yea, Josh. I don't have any family now. It's just me out here against the world."

"That's not true. You got me now! And I mean that."

"It's crazy, though, right? I mean, we hated each other! I know I hated you! I just never in a million years thought we'd be… friends. Don't make me regret saying this, but part of me feel glad about that, now."

I was at my most vulnerable, letting Josh in. It's crazy because at that moment, even knowing how much I lost that year, I felt like I gained so much more. I gained understanding, wisdom, and heart. I could tell Josh didn't exactly know how to respond. He just sat there bashfully, looking away. Then out of nowhere, he tensed up on me. I could tell that he had something heavy on his heart, so I asked,

"What is it?"

"Jesuse, there's something I need to tell you."

I waited for what felt like forever for him to open his mouth. He was making me nervous. Then suddenly, his wrinkled frown turned into a smile as he looked up at me and said,

"Your fly is open. Last one back to the car is a rotten egg!"

"A rotten egg? What the fuck? Are we back in first grade, now?"

Josh sprinted as fast as he could through the grass, making his way back to the mall's parking lot. I then grabbed my bag, put on my sprinting shoes, and I darted after him. Running with the wind blowing through my hair, I felt freer than ever. Like I was a little kid without a single worry in the world. I was ready to continue on my journey of healing and open a new chapter. I had no idea what I would do with my life, but I knew that I had all summer to figure it out. And though we all said our goodbyes to Lee Wallace High that day, I would soon to find out that Lee Wallace High wasn't exactly finished with us yet!

| 12 |

NEW BEGINNINGS

Tick Tock Tick Tock, the clock was running out! There I was kneeling behind a bush in front of Ms. Bloom's house, hoping like hell I wouldn't get caught. It was the day after graduation, and I'd taken my detective skills to a whole new level, and also with Jesuse accompanying me. I figured the odds of success would be in my favor. And I know, right, the nerve of me thinking I could win Jesuse over with a few laughs and adventure when I didn't even have the courage to be honest with him. *Honesty*, an essential part of any relationship, though I couldn't bring myself to tell him the truth. I just kept telling myself that when the moment was right, I'd have that conversation with him. In the meantime, however, I kept myself distracted with Melanie's case as I tried to bring down the real killer, Ms. Bloom.

You might be wondering how I figured it all out. Well, a little detective work and a short visit with Melanie at the county jail gave me everything I needed to condemn, Ms. Bloom. It was two weeks before graduation. Melanie finally agreed to meet with me after rejecting my visitation requests three times in a row. I guess with her; the fourth time was the charm. I had never been inside a jail before then, surprising, I know. So, I got pretty nervous when an officer walked me down the hall and told me to wait in a room with a glass window and green chair. The seat was hard and cold; it was early in the morning on a Saturday. I waited a minute or two before Melanie appeared before me on the other side of the glass. I waved like an idiot and smiled like one also. Melanie just gawked at me with repulsion. Then out of nervousness, I said to her,

"Hey, how's it going? Are you eating enough in here?"

I asked because she looked thinner from when I saw her last, and I didn't know how to start the conversation.

"How do you think it's going, Josh? I'm in jail! Look, the only reason I agreed to see you today was to tell you to your face to stop! Everyone else may be fooled by your act, but I'm not. You want to prove to everyone that you've changed, but I know who you really are! And you haven't changed a damn thing!"

"You're wrong about me. I'm not that person anymore. I don't think I ever really was. I'm here to help you, Melanie. I've been trying to solve this case, but I'm missing a big piece of the puzzle, and I need you to help me find it."

"What the hell is wrong with you? You're not a real detective. But my life, it's very real, and this is not a game. I don't have time to play make-believe with you."

"I'm not playing around. And actually, I've been applying to colleges that offer Criminal Justice program's so that I can pursue being a real cop, a detective. I think I finally found my niche."

"Wonderful! That's just what we need right now, more white male police officers."

"Look, I'm the good guy!"

"Ha, that's what they all said."

"Melanie, please. I can help you."

"No, you... How? Okay, how could you possibly help me?"

"By turning in the person that's responsible for James's murder."

"You don't even know who did it!"

"But you do!"

And right when I said those three words, she paused and just glared at me like a frightened little kitten. I wasn't even one hundred percent sure of what I was saying, not until that very moment.

"I don't know anything. You need to leave!"

"Why are you protecting her?"

"Protecting who?"

"You know who...Ms. Bloom?" I whispered.

"You don't know what you're talking about." Melanie sternly replied.

"No, I think I do. You may have half of the people at school convinced that you did this, but the other half of us believe otherwise. And I know that I've been an asshole to you. I'm sorry! Okay? I'm sorry! But don't throw your life away. I know that you're seeing her. Or at least was. And ever since you got arrested, she's been a completely different person. She did a good job hiding it from everyone else, but I could see past the make-up and fake smile right to her guilt.

I mean, come on, Melanie, do you really want to spend the rest of your life in prison for something you didn't do only to protect someone who'd let you?"

Melanie turned away from me, trying her best not to show emotion. I pleaded one last time for her to let me help. I could tell she was struggling with herself. I think that part of her was protecting Ms. Bloom. Why else wouldn't she be doing any and everything she could to clear her name? Melanie took one last long hard look at me before she got up, and said,

"Fine, Josh, you want to help? Look underneath the elephant trunk. I doubt that you'll be able to help, but who knows...maybe you're a better detective than I thought."

I didn't know if that was sarcasm or truth!

"Wait, Melanie! What elephant? Where?"

"You're the detective. Figure it out."

I watched the guard take Melanie out of the room, and I just continued sitting alone in deep confusion. It took me a week to figure out what, *underneath the elephant trunk*, meant. I didn't know if that was a metaphor or literal speaking. It wasn't until that following week, Monday afternoon, when I decided to follow Ms. Bloom home from school, that I began to understand. I made sure to park close to Ms. Bloom that morning to make it easier for me to follow her whenever she left for the day. I think by senior year, we all knew the makes and models of every teacher's vehicle, pretty dangerous, right?

Anyway, this particular Monday, I waited in my car for almost 45 minutes before watching Ms. Bloom head to hers. She was a complete mess, in a rush, with her bag overflowing with papers. Her hair was even a mess! But even through all of that, she was still banging. What! We all knew she was hot! I'm not going to deny that I found her attractive. But back to what happened next. I followed Ms. Bloom in my car, out of the parking lot, and down the street. She made three stops that day; one was to the post office, the other to the dry cleaners, and the last was at some nursing home. I was confused about that last stop. I always assumed she didn't have any family. So, I waited at this nursing home for what felt like an hour. Then when she finally came out, it was time to hit the road again.

It was around 5:40 P.M. when Ms. Bloom finally made arrived home. I parked down the street and watched as she rushed inside. I then got out of my car, walked along the sidewalk across the street, glaring at her house. I noticed stone fixtures right outside her house. By the way, Ms. Bloom's house was probably the best-looking house on the block. It was big, made of stone and wood, and she had a big front porch with a porch swing. I was just so mesmerized that I almost forgot what I was doing out there, that was until I noticed the elephant-shaped door handle on the front door of her house. It was then that I finally figured out what Melanie meant. And another week later, I was back. At first, Jesuse thought I was crazy, but I think he understood the more I explained it. So while we hid behind the bushes of her home, I filled Jesuse in on the plan.

"Okay, here's what's gonna happen. Once inside, I will need you to stand guard by the front door while I search the house for clues. If you see her or anyone pulling in, whistle!"

"Wait, whistle? I'm sorry, this is just too funny!"

"I'm serious!"

"Man, what kind of clues are you looking for, *Blues Clues?*"

"Ha! Very funny, Jesuse. I'm being serious! There might be something on her laptop or computer, an email, a file. I just need anything that will prove that she did it. Melanie told me to look under the elephant trunk!"

"The, what?"

"Never mind, just keep watch...please!"

Jesuse continued laughing himself red in the face as we made our way to the front porch. I knew that Ms. Bloom kept a spare key in one of her plants hanging above the front door, and I asked Jesuse to watch my back while I retrieved it. Alright, I may have followed Ms. Bloom more than once, okay! But after retrieving the key and unlocking the door, I gently placed it back in the pot, and we were finally inside.

"Wow, you really are taking this detective thing seriously, huh?"

"Yes, I told you! And, you know what, maybe part of me does feel like I have something to prove. Like, I have to work twice as hard at redeeming myself for all the messed-up shit I've done. But, if I can help Melanie, if I can be just a small reason why she breaks free, then maybe it'll mean that I'm not a total lost cause."

"You're a good guy Josh. I'm sure if she knew how hard you were trying, she'd see it too. Now, go find your clues. I'll guard the front door."

"Alright, man, thanks!"

The time was 9:46 A.M.; I could see the clock hanging on the wall in the living room from the doorway. Right as you walk inside, the stairwell is straight ahead, with the living room to the left and the dining room to the right with the kitchen just behind it. I immediately went up the stairs. I figured Ms. Bloom would keep her computer either in her bedroom or in an office room. The first room I checked was the bedroom. It was a large room with lots of windows that allowed the sun to shine straight through. I looked around for a computer or laptop, but I didn't see one, only a couple of dressers and her bed with an oversized red comforter on top. Ms. Bloom didn't even have a television in her room. Ha! Teachers!

After amusing myself, I decided to check inside her huge walk-in closet. There was enough room in there to fit a twin-sized bed and all of her clothes. I looked around, wondering to myself, how does a teacher afford a home like this? As much as they complain about not making enough money, it sure seemed like Ms. Bloom was making more than enough. And I must have gotten lost in her closet filled with perfectly hung skirts, dress shirts, and dresses because, by the time I walked back out to the center of the bedroom, I'd heard a voice calling out for me. I was startled as I turned around and saw Jesuse standing in the doorway.

"Dude! What are you doing? I told you to wait downstairs?"

"I'd been whistling for a good five minutes trying to get your attention and…"

"Wait, is she here?"

"No! You're fine. Take a breath. I figured I could help. Did you find anything?"

Before I could answer, Jesuse and I heard a loud thump

coming from across the hall. We freaked and hid behind the wall of Ms. Bloom's bedroom doorway. I stood on the right side, and Jesuse was on the left. Moments later, we heard a voice say,

"Hello? Jennifer, is that you?"

Jesuse and I then suddenly heard the door across the hall squeaking as it slowly opened. The voice became more precise, and the person continued to say,

"Hello? Who's there?"

"Dude, we need to get the hell out of here, now!" Jesuse whispered.

"Well, obviously! But we're kinda stuck right now?" I whispered back.

"There's not another way out of here?"

"No, just the walk-in closet and bathroom. Maybe you should hide in the closet, and I'll take the bathroom."

"Dammit, Josh!" Jesuse said in an angry whisper.

"What! How was I supposed to know she was hiding people in her house?" I whispered back.

We could hear the footsteps getting louder. I was sure whoever was on the other side of the wall was going to make their way inside and find us. I went to my right, and I motioned for Jesuse to go to his left toward the closet. As we tippy-toed away from the door, we heard a loud SLAM coming from downstairs. SHIT! That's when we bolted into our corners. I watched Jesuse run into the closet, and I hide in the shower. My heart was racing. I didn't know what was going to happen. Then I heard muffled voices as I stood anxiously in the shower with the curtain keeping me hidden. The muffling grew louder until I heard footsteps walking into the bathroom. That was it! My mission was over. I was dead!

I heard Ms. Bloom shouting out to the person who followed her into her room as she said, *I'll be out in a minute!* Then the bathroom door closed shut. Ms. Bloom and I were alone, in her bathroom! I was so nervous that I began to sweat. I tried to control my breathing, making sure that I was as quiet as a mouse. I then heard Ms. Bloom flop on the toilet and prayed that number one was all she had to do. After she finished relieving herself, I listened while she washed her hands. Ms. Bloom was almost on her way out the door when suddenly she stopped at the doorway. I worried if I made a noise, if maybe she could smell me, hell, I had no idea! But when Ms. Bloom started to walk back towards the shower, that's when I really began to freak! I could hear her footsteps getting closer, her breathing getting heavier, until she stopped, right in front of me. I was so sure Ms. Bloom would pull back the curtains! But instead, she turned around and quickly walked out of the bathroom.

Whew! I could finally breathe again. I listened for Ms. Bloom and her company to leave the room. Then, right when I was sure the coast was clear, I slowly stepped out of the shower and made my way back into the main bedroom. I then peeked into the hall as I walked past the doorway, and I heard Ms. Bloom talking to her company in the other room. That's when I darted into the closet where Jesuse was hiding to try and figure something out.

"Man, what the fuck? How are we supposed to get out of here?" Jesuse whispered.

"I don't know… I'm trying to come up with a plan."

"Damn! I really hope they teach you how to be a cop because you're really fucking this up. I mean, what were you doing in her bedroom anyway? Why didn't you search, I don't know, her office?"

"Because I thought that most people would keep their most valuable information in their bedrooms. I was going to check the office next. Look, let's just try to figure out a way to get out of here, okay!"

I pressed my ear against the closet door to see if I could hear anything, anyone, but it was quiet. I motioned for Jesuse to follow me as I led us back into the bedroom. By the time we reached the doorway, I had peeked my head into the hall to see if I could hear or see anything. Yet again, it was quiet. I figured they must have walked downstairs or gone into another room in the house. I then led Jesuse out into the hallway, and we began tippy-toeing our way back to freedom, that was until we paused at the top of the stairwell. We were seconds away from reaching the front door. Jesuse and I quietly looked over the stairs, ensuring the coast was clear before giving each other the clear to dart for it. Right before I took another step, I felt chills moving down my spine when I heard,

"EXCUSE ME! What the hell are you two doing in my house?"

Immediately, we turned around, and Ms. Bloom was standing right behind us. She continued making her way towards us with her hands folded across her chest in deep rage. Standing just three feet in front of us, she asked once more,

"I asked you two a question! What the hell are you doing in my house?"

I had to say something. It was my idea anyway, my fault we got caught. I just sucked it up and said,

"We know it was you!"

"Excuse me?" She asked.

"How long are you going to let Melanie rot behind bars for something that you did? We know the truth, Ms. Bloom. About everything!"

"Is that right?"

"Jennifer, what's going on? Who are these people?"

That's when Jesuse and I saw an older man with a cane walking out the room, the room across from Ms. Bloom's. We both assumed it was her father until she shouted out in vexation,

"Go back to your room. I'll be there in a second!"

We waited for the strange older man to walk back into his room after eyeing Jesuse and me with skepticism. I then looked to Ms. Bloom and said,

"I don't plan on leaving here without something that'll put you away!"

"Josh, stop!" Jesuse blurted.

"You know, it's bad enough that you took away her innocence, but now you want to take away her freedom? You're seriously fucked up in the head for that. But it's alright; I'm not stopping until Melanie is free and you're the one rightfully behind bars. So, you might want to go and tell your dad or whoever the hell he is that you'll be longer than just a second."

Ms. Bloom then began to laugh, almost hysterically, while

I stood there mute. I was confused because I didn't find anything funny at all. She then took another step closer, looked at me, and said,

"That man is not my father...no, that man is my rapist! And the thing that I find most funny is that he can't remember a damn thing! The man you just saw looking dazed and confused, who can barely walk, has Alzheimer's. He raped me for nearly ten years of my childhood and has no idea! Talk about stealing someone's innocence? Trust me; no one understands that better than me. And now, almost 20 years later, he shows up on my doorstep begging me for shelter, me! The world doesn't need your horrible detective skills to solve this case, Josh. I've already made up my mind that I'd turn myself in. I just wanted to make sure that the damn man would have a nice nursing home to go to before I did. And you're right, I guess I am a little fucked up, but at least I'm not afraid to admit it...

"My love for Melanie was and still is the realest thing in my heart. She is the only reason why I'm turning myself in. I couldn't bear the thought of showing up in her life twenty years later and not remember the pain I've caused. I'd rather fix it now while I still have the chance. Because although trying to forgive someone who has wrong you is difficult, forgiving someone who can't remember it is almost impossible. And yet, here I am. Well, we all hit rock bottom at some point in our lives. However, I can promise you both that your time will be coming. With that said, I suggest the two of you get the hell out of my house, now, because the last time I checked, breaking and entering was still a crime."

"How do I know you're telling the truth? How do I know that you'll turn yourself in?" I asked.

"Well, I guess you won't know. But my home security footage will be all the proof that the REAL detectives need! Now, go!"

"Come on, Josh…" Jesuse begged.

That was the last time I saw Ms. Bloom. She stood there lifeless with sheer sadness and anger in her eyes. I could tell that she needed a release. I mean, to hold something that painful and profound, to carry a secret like that, must be a pretty lonely way to live. Part of me felt terrible as I walked down the staircase and out the door. It's crazy how you think you can know someone, judge them, but not even come close to understanding their core. After hearing Ms. Bloom speak, I was convinced that she believed she loved Melanie. I only hoped that Ms. Bloom would do the right thing and that I'd get better at being a detective. I mean, I wasn't that bad, was I? I figured a lot of it out on my own, but I think Jesuse was right. I should've checked the freaking office first. Either way, I did my best, and all I could do was wait, hope, and pray that everything would be okay.

NOTHING was okay! Everything about my newly found hell was devastatingly NOT OKAY! For a very, and I do mean, very brief time in my life, I felt a tiny speckle of happiness. I felt absolute joy, laughter, comfort, and even love. The darkness in my life was no longer the center of my existence. Light had finally reached me, and I took comfort in knowing that my darkest days would be behind me. Darkness, however, can't be contained forever. Eventually, it finds a way of sucking up your light by forcing you to lose the happiness, comforts, and joys that life occasionally brings. So, I say, hold on tight to yours while you can. I sure as hell wish that I had. I lost two loves. I felt like I had also lost my new best friend and my old one, and then I lost the one person I cherished most in this world. I found myself truly alone, destined to spend the next 30 years of my life in a women's correctional facility in Indianapolis, all because I didn't fight for myself. Instead, I allowed myself to get bullied by monsters who would coerce me into a plea that they knew I wasn't guilty of.

But someone needed Justice. And Justice, whether just or not, is what they were going to get. You know, I thought the worst part of all of this was finding out that Gabrielle went back to dick, but no, it wasn't that. The worst part was not graduating with my friends, not putting on my cap and gown, and walking across the stage wearing the biggest and brightest smile ever. It felt like my life was over, and in a way, I started accepting the fact that my fate would be glued to metal bars for eternity. After Gabrielle told me that she could no longer see me, I think that was the first time I lost hope. Ms. Bloom was never going to do the right thing. How could she? Why would she? It was graduation day, and the only person who came to see me that day was Ms. Bailey.

I begged her not to come, though, because I knew that she wasn't feeling well. I worried about her stressing and having to be at two places: the jail with me and then at graduation with everyone else. Ms. Bailey, though, never let any obstacle get in her way. She came to see me just two hours before the graduation ceremony. It was hard, probably one of the most challenging days for me being in there. I remember Ms.

Bailey sitting across from me wearing this fancy feathered dove-colored blouse and a black knee-high skirt. She looked gorgeous; I just smiled and felt like for a second that everything would be okay.

"You look extremely nice for graduation Ms. Bailey. Are you hiding a hot date around the corner or in your car somewhere?" I smiled.

"No, Melanie! I wish! I just wanted to feel good today. Is that okay with you? I had to find a way to keep the spirit of hope alive."

"Well, hope, looks really good on you. And you sound better too. So I guess it was just some kind of flu?"

I didn't entirely believe that what she had was the flu, but the lie was much easier to accept than the truth, as you know.

"Y-Yeah! And you know what? I feel better too!"

I knew Ms. Bailey better than she thought, or maybe she was aware of how well I knew her too. Because after hearing that reply, which I was partly skeptical of in the first place, the two of us had an emotional exchange that was more powerful than words. I didn't know what was going on with her, but I knew she wasn't ready to tell me the truth. Which is why I left things at,

"Good! I'm glad."

"Listen, Melanie, I- I came here to tell you that...I think you should talk to your mother. And before you get upset, just hear me out. I'm not always going to be around. And I need to know that no matter what happens to me, that you, Melanie you, will be okay. I understand that your mother has done horrible things to you in the past and even recently, but I think it's time for you to walk through your pain. Yes, forgiving is so much easier said than done, but if you at least try a little, day by day, you'll find that it starts to work."

"Why...why are you saying all of this? Where is this coming from?"

"Your mother has been calling me every day, begging me to convince you to see her or accept at least one of her calls. I'm not here to advocate for her. I just understand human imperfection. I see it in your mom, myself. And yes, even Ms. Bloom."

"Wait, what do you mean? Why did you say, Ms. Bloom?"

Well, that sure woke me up! I didn't understand why she'd be mentioning imperfections and Ms. Bloom in the same sentence unless she knew something. And apparently, she did know something because soon after questioning Ms. Bailey, she gave me this humble smirk after batting her eyes. I tried to play it off, pretending I didn't understand, but the smile that shortly formed across my face was the icing on the cake.

"It took a while for me to see it, but yes, I know Melanie. I know everything, which is the reason why I'm sitting here trying to have this conversation with you now. You're still hurting. And, of course, you are. You should be! Your own mother tried to kill you! Don't you think that it's time to have that conversation with her? To make her carry some of that weight?"

"I can't...she doesn't think she did anything wrong. How can I even begin to forgive her when she's not even sorry?"

"Just talk to her. I promise you won't have anything to lose."

Ms. Bailey smiled, reassuring me that everything would be okay. Part of me was confused about why she wasn't upset with me after knowing about my relationship with Ms. Bloom. It troubled me, and so I had to ask,

"So you're not mad at me. I mean, you're not going to yell at me or call me foolish?"

"My first reaction was to, yes! But I can't judge you, Melanie, or her; it's not my place. I think you've both suffered enough in life without me adding my judgments to it. We, as people...we, tend to lead with anger in these situations rather than with love. Inside every person lies an origin story. And in each story lies a villain. I think the purpose or the point of that is finding a way to overcome while coming out on the other side a stronger, wiser, and kinder person."

"You said that we both suffered in life, how do you mean? How has she suffered?"

"I think that's something you should ask her yourself... should the opportunity ever present itself. But right now, I just want you to focus on getting out of here. You have so much life to live and so many more people to inspire."

"What do you mean? I never inspired anyone."

"Of course you have! You inspired me. You might think that your presence in this world doesn't make a difference to the lives of the people around you, but it does... it has! I can see it. And if you don't remember anything else, I want you to remember and understand that you are loved, Melanie. Your life, your existence, matters! And there is no one else like you on this planet who can bring the kind of joy you bring. You're an orchid! And I'm so happy, Melanie, to have had the chance to love you."

The words Ms. Bailey used to describe me, I never felt more loved, more alive than I did at that moment. I didn't realize what I needed until I was receiving it. Ms. Bailey was right; I was still hurting. By standing up to my mother, talking to her, I thought that I had somehow moved on, but healing doesn't quite work that way. At least mine didn't. So, I decided that I would see my mom, after all, one final time. I was due to leave for Indianapolis two days after graduation. So, the next day after I visited with Ms. Bailey, I was ready to see my mother.

But right after visiting with Ms. Bailey, I spent the rest of the day brainstorming in my mind what I would say to my mother, the questions I would ask when I'd see her. There was only one real question that I needed to have answered. But how does one ask such a question? I wasn't sure. What I was sure of was that I'd be spending the rest of my life in prison unless someone decided to stop being self-centered and confessed. Who was I kidding though, if she didn't say anything after three months, why would she now? I spent the rest of the day until early morning in a daze. I barely slept through the night! I think part of me was going to miss the comforts of my small cage. I had no idea of what stresses would come with a larger one, let alone the kind of women who'd be waiting for me. The area where I stayed was small, with about six cells inside. We all shared the common area and a small TV that sat in the corner of the wall. The women inside mostly kept to themselves, as did I. Which made it easier on me when I finally was able to dream.

When morning rolled around, and it was almost time for me to see my mother, I became filled with such heavy nerves that I think I gave myself an extreme case of the runs. TMI? Well, I counted the hours and minutes until the clock read

9:30 A.M. I guess I was more nervous about my visit with my mother than I was over going to prison! But it was finally time for me to address her, to be brave, and demand answers. Minutes later, a guard called my name and walked me out of my cell to the room where I had my other visits. I took a deep breath as I sat down, ensuring my edges were intact and my sweater was free of wrinkles. Then before I knew it, there my mother was, on the other side of the glass, taking a seat. She wore a light grey leather jacket and black jeans. I was surprised to see her looking so well. Of course, I didn't let her know that I noticed. I just waited for my mother to get her greetings out of the way and say,

"It's strange seeing you on that side of this glass. How does it feel?"

"What do you mean, how does it feel? I'm innocent! That's how it feels."

"Then why did you plead guilty?"

"I don't want to talk about that. What I do want to talk about is you pretending to give a damn about me when we both know that you don't!"

"That's not true! I may not have shown it in the best ways possible, but I do love you."

"How? How can you sit there and say that you love me when... after you tried to kill me? And please don't blame it on the alcohol or drugs or your mental illness."

"I don't know what you want me to say, Melanie. I wasn't in my right mind. Mental illness goes much deeper than you think."

"This wasn't about you having some kind of psychotic break! What did I do to you that would allow you to think that the way you treated me was okay? Because it wasn't just one instance, it was many. Damn near every day of my life was hell because of you. So just tell me, why did you never love me?"

"Okay, you think you can handle the truth. Here it is. Your brain... it's funny! And you turning out to be a-a-dike, wasn't the only reason I couldn't love you... you were never even supposed to be born! I wasn't ready to be a mother. And my parents, they were devoted Christians... loyal to God! Hell, I think they loved Jesus more than they loved me. But getting pregnant and having a baby out of wedlock, well, that wasn't acceptable. I became the family fuck up, the shameful black sheep. And when you were born, even watching you grow up, I knew that something was wrong with you, that you were different. I couldn't even bring you around my family...

"And I didn't want to! I didn't want them to think that I was... that I had anything to do with how you turned out. When I was pregnant with you, my mother refused to have any kind of relationship with me. And when she died, I didn't even get an invite to her funeral. I didn't know that she had passed away until months later! The only person I had in my life was your dad whenever he decided to stay in town for longer than a week at a time. But even then, I don't think I had him either. I had no one in my corner, no one that loved me, except for you, but hated you! I resented you, and I blamed you, and I'm sorry, but it's just how I felt."

"It's just how you felt? No... it's how you feel... And to think that I was trying to work up in my funny brain a way to forgive you. But after hearing you speak, knowing that you not only hate me for existing but that you also hate who I am, I can't forgive that. So I guess at least now I know the truth. And I know that it's not just all in my *funny brain*. But you were wrong about something. There is nothing wrong with me! I am exactly the way God made me. And you and I both know that God doesn't make any mistakes. But the only mistake that happened here is that you missed out on being loved by someone incredible. I do have one question, though, while we're on the topic. If God loves all his children and for who they are, just the way they are, why can't you love yours?"

I was devastated. That truth was difficult to accept. Seconds later, I called for the guard to take me back, and I left my mother sitting alone with her thoughts. I was distraught for the rest of the day. Before we had that conversation, I could excuse her behavior based on her wires not being properly connected. But hearing that truth forced me to start the healing process all over again. Would I have preferred that she lied? No... I only wished that she loved me unconditionally. But maybe instead of hoping that she one day would, I could have been loving myself more. Perhaps if I learned to love myself enough, then I'd love enough for the both of us. After crying myself to sleep that night, I woke up the next morning with red puffy eyes. I didn't even get much of a warning. The guards just rushed inside and told me it was time to go. And as I made my way outside, I desperately looked around, waiting for someone to shout out that I was free to go, but nobody ever called for me. I just stepped my way onto the bus and left behind the only people I've grown to know.

Then as the bus slowly departed, I began to feel that same

rumbling in my stomach that I felt before the visit with my mother. All I could do was sit back in my seat and listen to the growling in my stomach grow louder. The sad reality I came to face was that I wouldn't be saved from my horrible fate no matter how much I prayed. I was so tired and so cold on that bus that I ended up taking a short nap. By the time I woke, we had arrived in Indianapolis at the prison. I sat up in my seat, rubbed my eyes, and prepared myself for the next 30 years of my life. As I stepped off the bus, I was escorted inside by one of the correctional officers. Getting checked in was, well, excruciating. The uniforms the women wore weren't like what I thought they'd be. And the environment there compared to the jail was like day and night. I couldn't even settle into my unit without someone taking an issue with me, bumping into me, or calling me a bitch. *Jesus Christ*, nobody gave me the handbook on surviving PMS in prison!

Then once I was finally inside my unit, my new home, I was greeted by two women. One was older, African American, standing by the bunk, and the other was young and Caucasian, resting on top of the bunk. There were two sets of bunk beds; both connected in the shape of an L. The older woman then approached me and said,

"You can take the top bunk over there. We're a quiet group in here, don't worry, baby. And whatcha looking so scared for? We won't bite! We might poke and stab a little from time to time but won't hurt you unless we have to."

The two of them started laughing, and I didn't know whether to join in or run.

"Relax, baby; I was just playing around. But, I mean,

Tiffany over there, she might bite. And she might nibble too, so watch out!"

"Oh, shut up!" Tiffany replied.

"So, what's your name?" I asked.

"Oh Damn, I said hello to you and everything else but forgot to introduce myself. I'm Tracy! And you are?"

"I'm Melanie." I smiled nervously.

"Well, welcome to Hell, Melanie. I hope your stay will be short! Oh, and hey, do you have to pee?"

"No, I'm fine."

"Okay, well, I do! So come with me, I'll show you around."

As I started to follow Tracy, Tiffany got off her bunk and said,

"Hey Tracy, they're going to start doing construction in the shower rooms. You should ask them to build you a bed right over the toilet. That way, you'll never have to get off again."

"Oh, Fuck you, Tiffany."

"I swear, woman…you spend more time on the toilet than you do anywhere else!"

The two of them continued joking and teasing each other before Tracy realized she just couldn't hold her bladder any longer. She then tugged on my shirt and ordered me to follow. As I followed Tracy down the hall, she gave me the 411 on all the drama inside the prison. She went on for miles. Then once we were inside the restroom area, I waited for Tracy by the doorway while she continued yakking away. Suddenly, I was shoved by one of the women entering the room. I didn't think much of it at the time; it seemed to be a tradition around there. But when I found myself being boxed in by a group of four, the sound of Tracy's voice faded away as the sound of my heartbeat increased through my eardrums.

The woman who stood directly in front of me, and I do mean centimeters away from me, smiled and asked,

"Hey, you're Monica's kid, right?"

"Uh, yeah! I mean, why? Do you know her?"

"Yeah, we know her alright. She was kind of important around here. A lot of people respected her."

"That's...nice!" I dryly replied.

What else could I say? From the overpowering masculinity, I sensed that my mother didn't exactly leave a good impression.

"Yeah, well, we'll see you around, Monica's daughter."

Finally, the women freed me from their cloud of enhanced testosterone, and I could breathe again. They walked back out of the shower room, leaving me more terrified than when I first walked through the prison doors. Shortly after, Tracy came out of the stall and glared at me with bewilderment. She warned me that those women were not to be messed with, that they were dangerous! I figured my mother might have made a couple of friends while she was in the big house, but not once did I consider the number of enemies she must have racked up. Later that evening, I was assigned to clean up duty in the kitchen with a few other women. I was in the dish room making mop water to mop the floors when I heard a loud slam coming from the door behind me. It was the same group of women I just saw in the shower room earlier. I looked around and realized that I was the only person left in the dish room from my group, and I panicked.

The room itself was a decent size. It had two large sink areas on opposite sides of each other with one dish dryer. There was even a small closet inside the room. I stood with my back towards the water hose where the mop bucket sat, waiting for the women to surround me like sharks in a typhoon. It was five of them this time, and by the looks on their faces, I knew they weren't there to welcome me with loving arms. So then, the more masculine woman once again was standing centimeters away from me, glaring deep into my eyes. I didn't know what to do. The neurons in my brain were firing at an alarming rate. It was so fast that I didn't have time to think of an escape. But there was no escape!

"I promise, I'll make this quick." She said.

That was the last thing I heard before my body became their piñata. It was one swing right after the other. The women started with my torso, then my ribs, and then finally my face as I fell unconsciously to the ground. They say life is full of surprises. Well, this was one giant surprise that I did not see coming. A little warning would have been nice, *mother!* But she couldn't even do that. And knocking me to the ground wasn't going to be enough to stop them. No, they wanted to see blood! I was coming in and out of consciousness the entire time, and all I could hear through my distorted eardrums was,

"Stop, Zee, that's enough. We were supposed to rough her up a little, not kill her!"

I guess one of them had a conscience. But even that wasn't enough to save me. Zee had to take one final swing to my temporal lobe before she finally tired herself out. The ringing in my ears and the colors dancing over my eyes were enough to let me know that I became paralyzed. I couldn't speak, and I couldn't move. But eventually, those colors turned into a bright light, and that light became the only thing I could see. Then, with my body stretched across the floor, profusely bleeding from my skull, I went back to my happiest memories. The very first night, Ms. Bailey took me in, and we ate ice cream until I could feel my stomach about to burst. The first time I met Renee, and she offered me her lunch because she knew that I didn't have anything to eat. I saw and remembered everyone, and for a moment, I could finally feel the love I had surrounding me. It's true what people say; you don't realize what you have until you're about to lose it.

I learned that we perform through our tragedies wearing different masks to disguise our pain for happiness. But it's like I said before; life for me has been one long, never-ending matinee. And although I was the star, it seemed that death found me first. And right before my curtains closed one final time, I saw an angel! It was a beautiful, strong, vibrant angel that had appeared before me. As I began to see her face, tears welled up in my eyes because I knew that death had found her too. But she welcomed death as the new beginning by extending her arm out to me and smiling,

"Come on, Melanie, it's time to go."

"Where are we going?"

"Home!"

Home! It's funny... Throughout my entire existence on Earth, I never truly knew what home was. Not until Ms. Bailey opened her heart to me. Love like that, her wisdom and kindness, it's rare. But when you find that it touches you, listen and follow in its footsteps. You'll be surprised by how far it'll take you. And yes, there was a time when I wondered; *what's the point of life if it ends in death?* But I think I finally got the answer to my question when Ms. Bailey extended out her hand to me. After that, the only thing left for me to do was to grab ahold tight and let light carry me through, leaving behind everyone I loved. There was just one tiny problem, though. I wasn't quite ready to say goodbye…